The Clashing of Two Swords

of Two

Renee Fotch

WestBow
PRESS
A DIVISION OF THOMAS NELSON

WestBow Press books may be ordered through booksellers or by contacting:

WestBow Press
A Division of Thomas Nelson
1663 Liberty Drive
Bloomington, IN 47403
www.westbowpress.com
1 (866) 928-1240

ISBN: 978-1-4908-1655-5 (sc)
ISBN: 978-1-4908-1656-2 (hc)
ISBN: 978-1-4908-1654-8 (e)

Library of Congress Control Number: 2013921378

Printed in the United States of America.

WestBow Press rev. date: 12/13/2013

Dedication

I would like to dedicate this Book to my one true Love and that is the Holy Spirit. Without Him there is no creative ability or gift to be able to write such a book. You are the love and passion of my life. My wedding dress is washed and ready and I am waiting for the day I become your bride.

I would love to say many thanks to those who have influenced me, built me up and supported me in this incredible venture.

I would like to say a BIG thank you to Debbie Chappell, my sweetest, dearest, best and most inspirational friend in this world! You have always been my biggest fan Debbie, loving me through thick and thin. Always inspiring me to go higher, believing in me to be more than the ordinary. Your love and support to me cannot be measured here on this earth. The ministry we have done together that states in Mathew 10, has been over the top! We have killed snakes and shut the mouths of lions together. You are "Mary" at heart, always seeking the heart of his presence above all. You are beautiful inside and out! Thank you with all my heart, I love you deeply, you too Wayno.

I would also like to say a HUGE thank you to Nora Robbins, my twin in so many ways. I have learned leaps and bounds from you. You truly are a Mighty woman of God! You are a skilled Sword fighter, able to take down the Leviathan's we face and cut off their heads. You can see the invisible and make it materialize in this life, I love that! You provoke me to be great, to excel, to believe "Nothing" is Impossible, and to soar on the wings of the wind. Together our prayers have stormed the gates of Hell crashing them to the floor. You have denied this world and risen above the torrential tides to a higher life style. Thank you! You're a rare black pearl, hidden away in Him, to come out uniquely set apart for a divine purpose. I love you and count it an honor to call you my true sister!

Mom and Dad, you two together have encouraged me to look through different glasses in this life. You have taught me to believe beyond the normal, to be bold as a lion, to take chances and to love until it cuts deep. You have encouraged me to take the narrow road in life and to not be conformed by this world, but rather push toward the goal of the high calling in Christ. You have taught me to not except mediocre as acceptable. Your faith has stretched mine in ways you will never know. I love that you have instilled in me to read, eat and sleep the Word of God. I truly would not be where I am today without you! You two are my inspiration!

Thank you to my sweet sisters Robin and Kim and brothers Bob and Shawn my precious family. The love that I have for you guys keeps me motivated in my faith. You are all leaders, able to conquer cities by your character. I love you all endlessly! Then there is Tammy, Deborah, Karen, Deb M, Deb R, Lisa W, and my Faith Harvest Family in whom you all keep me accountable to always press upward.

Last but not least there is my Labradootle Lollipop. You are the one who waited patiently while I wrote this book. Still loving me when I wouldn't play when I came home! Your love is so unconditional, you're just like God! Your name matches you perfectly, you're so sweet! You are my watch dog, sounding the battle cry when an enemy comes near my home. You're truly a girl's best friend!

Nahum 3:3 "The cavalry attacks— they will charge ahead; their swords will be flashing and their spears will glimmer! There will be many slain; there will be piles of the dead, and countless casualties--so many dead that we will stumble over the corpses."

When Light and Darkness collide the
sound is heard in the heavens as

The Clashing of Two
SWORDS

Contents

1 – The Bloody Nose

Before I begin, I would like to introduce you to five amazing women whom you will find throughout the pages of this book: Jean, Anne, Lynn, Marie and me.

Early in February 2010 the five of us planned a trip overseas. It was there that we set up a pillar in the middle of the Jordan River in memory of the wildest, hardest, and greatest time of all of our Christian lives! This pillar is branded upon our minds and hearts, and we will never, ever forget it!

The Bible is called by many titles. Let me name just a few: The Gospel, The Truth, The Word of God, The Holy Scriptures, The Law of the Lord, The Scroll, The Living Word of God, and the one that we will be speaking about throughout this book The Sword of the Spirit. The Bible says that this Sword is alive and active and it cuts down enemy strongholds. We have weapons, not seen with the human eye, but we do have them and they are very powerful!

We landed on a very narrow runway to a remote Island. Then we had a three hour drive to the city where we would be spending the next seventeen days together. This book is all about those exciting days. So sit back and, hold on tightly to your drink, because you are going on one of the most terrifying adventures ever recounted to date.

Ricky and Reba, the pastor and his wife, met us at the airport to take us on that long way back to their home. Reba sat with us in the back of a small, open ended, white pickup truck. She started to share with us a story about four young ladies who were all sisters. Although I wanted to hear what she had to say, I was only half listening: we'd been traveling for twenty-one hours and; we were exhausted.

Reba started off by saying that these ladies were eagerly awaiting our arrival from the United States because they had heard that we had the power to deliver them. "Deliver?" I thought. "Seriously?" My spirit quickly woke up within me, and she now had my undivided attention. Reba went on to explain. Lisa, Carla, Lila, and Jenny's mother had gone off to Israel to work for about two years. Their father could not take care of them as he had wanted, so he turned them over to his sister to raise.

Now, here is where the story all begins. I will take you into the middle of a snake pit. Stay alert and read slowly to see if there is any way possible that you may have been bitten by a viper and never even realized it.

So where were we? Oh, yes: now the only bad part about the aunt raising these girls was that she was a witch! Yes, I said "Witch!" Of course no one realized that she was a witch, as she pretty much acted like everyone else. She did not come with a broom in her hand and wearing a black hat. Oh, no! She attended a church and blended right in. This church, however, was a little different from the ones to which we are all accustomed to. This church was for all of those who claimed to be mediums.

The Bible tells us, "These are called false apostles, transforming themselves into apostles of Christ. For Satan transforms himself into an angel of light. His servants also masquerade as servants of righteousness." (2 Corinthians 11: 13-15).

One day while their aunt was in her unique prayer time, or séance, she pulled up from the invisible realm of trolls or dwarfs, which are all evil spirits. They suddenly appeared in the room in which she was sitting in. When she saw the spirits come into the room, she asked them to follow each one of her nieces throughout their lives. Then, she called each girl to her side in turn and gave her this spirit guide to accompany her wherever she went.

Are you thinking what I was thinking? The girls saw black, evil spirits and liked them? Yes, they did, but they were not black, as we think they'd be. No, they were white and friendly, just like the Scripture says; "Satan himself masquerades as an angel of light." (2 Corinthians 11:14) Black spirits would have sent them running away in fear.

These young girls grew up and went on to live normal lives, right? Well, if normal is having a troll follow you throughout your everyday affairs, then yes! Of course they were the only ones who could see these spirits, because it took faith to make them alive. The energy the aunt created in the room empowered the spirits to come alive and become active. Remember what the apostle says, "Faith is: the substance of things hoped for and the evidence of things not yet seen." (Hebrews 11: 1) Whatever you put your faith in will, eventually, materialize. Once alive, these dwarfs would materialize and hold the girl's hands to comfort them while their mom was away.

Many years had gone by. The girls, now ladies in their twenties, had all started going to a Christian church. Each one had now asked Jesus Christ and the Holy Spirit to come and live inside of them. Swishhhhhhhhhhhhh was the sound of SWORDS clashing together! Of course they were heard only in the spirit realm, because light and darkness were now colliding with great force!

Heaven and Hell were meeting once again with drawn Swords, just like the day Satan was cast out of Heaven, because WAR was brewing! Their bodies were violently convulsing from the spiritual jolt of electricity shooting through them, because Light and Darkness had come head to a head!

These ladies had no idea of what was going on inside of them. The Evil spirits that were masquerading as white angels were now unveiled as black monsters! The pale hands that once held them close to their sides now became black, scaly claws, grasping at their souls for safety. These unseen snarling wolves had found a home and were not intending to leave without a fight. A fight only won in the spirit realm.

Ephesians 6:10 tells us to put on God's armor, the armor of a heavy-armed soldier that God supplies, so that we can successfully stand up against all the strategies and the deceits of the devil. Then we go to war, because we don't put on armor to stay indoors and cower in a corner. No, we are in a wrestling match, a battle not with humans, but against the despotisms, against the powers, against the master spirits who are the world's rulers in this present darkness, against the spirit forces of wickedness in the heavenly, supernatural sphere.

When we put this armor on, then we are ready! Ready to fight and to resist the enemy, standing our ground on the evil day of danger, and having done all the crisis demands, we stand firmly in our place through Christ Jesus.

Once the girls became Christians and gave their lives to God, the battle began. Light and darkness were battling for position, and light was going to win!

If we walk into a dark room and turn on the light, darkness has no choice but to run and hide, because light rules over darkness! The Bible says in Jeremiah 23:24, that God's Holy Spirit covers the whole earth: "Can any hide himself in secret places that I shall not see him?" It's kind of like cold water poured on a burning frying pan: little bubbles rise up, run and scatter!

Every time we see a demonic spirit at work in the life of a person, it is either through the soul (the mind) or the body. In Luke 13:16, it says, "Should not this woman, a daughter of Abraham, whom Satan has kept bound for eighteen long years, be set free on the Sabbath day from what bound her?" If we open a door to the enemy he will come in. When we open, the door to our homes and leave them wide open will thieves not eventually come in and rob us?

Although these sisters were young and innocent of recognizing danger, it did not change the fact that they were now in a bind. They had come to the place in their lives where they did not need as much help with the spirit guides as they had when they were younger. As a result, the spirit guides did not materialize like they had in the past. Little did they know, however, that these monster spirits did not leave, but made residence inside of each one of them. They were lying dormant like an evil disease.

The enemy preys on the helpless as the psalmist says, "His mouth is full of lies and threats; trouble and evil are under his tongue. He lies in wait near the villages; from ambush he murders the innocent. His eyes watch in secret for his victims; like a lion in cover he lies in wait. He lies in wait to catch the helpless; he catches the helpless and drags them off in his net." (Psalm 10:7-9)

It is terrible how he catches us unaware and pounces on the innocent, before they have done anything wrong. I once saw a You Tube video that showed a troop of buffalo. They were all grazing on the grass when a little baby wandered away to a greener patch of ground. The buffalo had no idea that in the tall grass a pride of lions was hiding. Their eyes were fixed and their bodies were all at a stance to see the little one helpless, and oblivious to anything around it. That's when they went in for the kill. The Bible says, "Pride comes before destruction, and a haughty spirit before a fall." Proverbs 16:18.

Now they were all adults and attending a church, they had no idea that darkness had taken up residence inside of their souls. They were so scared about what was happening to them. That's when they made a desperate call to Reba and Ricky for help. Something we were getting ready to do.

This is where we come in, a Methodist, a Baptist and three Pentecostals Charismatics. We had to throw all of our doctrinal teachings out the window, because this was what we called RAW Christianity. No amount of teaching could prepare us for what was to come.

Here in the good ol' USA we rarely hear of this kind of thing, right? I looked at Anne, who was sitting next to me, and said, "Cool, are you ready for this?!" She looked like she was going to pass out from exhaustion, but I saw her sit up straight and boldly say "Yes I am!" Gulp?

Just then, blood started gushing out of my nose like a volcano erupting. A bloody nose! Really? We scurried to find something, anything to stop it! It came out of nowhere! That's when we knew, not how, but who! We weren't scared, just very aware of his devices to try and stop us, so we started to pray. We prayed for angels around the truck we were riding in. Then we prayed for safety for everyone back in the USA. The Enemy knew his TIME WAS UP. He was going to have to vacate his home, as he had heard us planning this Power Trip way were back in the United States months earlier. He was running scared! The interesting thing is, I NEVER get bloody noses, I mean NEVER!

2 - Kleenex

When we arrived at our destination it was very late Friday night, so we slept for a few hours before the morning light came in. The next morning we got dressed and went out early with Ricky and Reba. They had scheduled for us to speak at various bible studies, church services, and to do street evangelism.

Although the sun was shining, a dreary blackness was in the air right above us. It had been raining for several hours, but this had now diminished to a faint sprinkling. The smog had set in just low enough to the ground, to give us a very chilling mystery novel. Ricky and Reba led us through dingy dark alley ways, winding and winding around stones, crevices and muddy filled potholes. We swatted flies everywhere we went, until finally we reached the place we would reside, a big open space of land. This is where we would feed hungry children who would come with a spoon and bowl in hand. In the United States, a small group of us help support these wonderful provisions of meals. With our funds we feed about three hundred malnourished children, four times a month. Of course we would love to do more, but our funds are limited.

We were so excited because Reba and her team were letting us help fill the children's bowls! They had diligently prepared a hearty chicken pastry soup for the children to eat the evening before. They had told the children to get into a long line, which wrapped around their homes and then back into the street. This was very emotional as little children made their way through the line to us. This was the only meal they would receive all week, to the best of our knowledge.

They held out their bowls when it was their turn to receive some food. Once they got their meal, they all sat down on the ground and said a special prayer of thanks to God.

Personally I cannot imagine only eating once a week. This tears my heart out, thinking this is what these children do. They would come with their heads hanging low, barely catching eye contact with us because of shame or despair.

It stands as a great reminder of, the importance of good nutrition for an all-round good disposition: It was clear that their spirits inside of them were also affected by a lack of food, leaving them sad and depressed.

Some of us do that very same thing every week in the United States: Our spirit inside is what keeps us nourished on the outside as well. When we only go to church on Sunday morning, and then never pick up another morsel of spiritual food until the next Sunday Church service, we are starving on the inside and it affects our outside character. Jesus has the answer for this dilemma of malnourishment. It's called His Word. He says, "I stand at the door and knock; if anyone hears and listens to and heeds My voice and opens the door, I will come in to him and will eat with him, and he will eat with Me. (Revelations 3:20)

We watched as a little girl received her bowl of food. She would not eat until her little brother had gotten his too. When they both got their food, she got up and they took it home. I had asked the helpers why they did not stay with the rest of the children. They told me that there were other siblings at home and that their mom and dad had not eaten either, and so they waited to get their meals so they could take it home to the rest of their family.

It really is better to give than to receive, because the greatest blessing always falls on the one who gives. However, this blessing was hard to receive for many reasons. I don't mean to sound belittling to what we were doing to help them; it was just that it seemed so little, to such a big problem. It felt like we were just putting a Band-Aid on a broken leg.

All I know is that we walked away from that day with a box of Kleenex in hand. I kept reflecting on how we spend our money, and what we could do to feed more.

The Bible says "Whoever is kind to the poor, lends to the Lord, and he will reward them for what they have done." Wow, what a verse, let's lend to God! (Proverbs 19:17)

After the feedings we decided to rest for a while. I was the first on bat at speaking the next morning and needed to look over my notes before I started to snooze.

3 - Forgiven

I awoke yawned, coffeed up and stumbled to the church, where I spoke on forgiveness. God had moved so very powerfully upon many of the people that came to hear the message. One thing I know is that un- Forgiveness is the enemy's number one way of keeping people in bondage. He thrives in keeping hatred and discord alive in the church, among friends and in the intimate core of most families. This message was the beginning of a very interesting night.

Ricky and Reba have a Bible study in their home every Sunday night. People were coming into the house to just relax and reflect on the service from that morning. They all started to share testimonies about their lives, and how God had spoken to them in the morning service. A few of them shared stories that were so deep with emotional trauma that it was hard for them to speak about it, without a continuous flood of tears. Although they found it very difficult to forgive all those that had done them wrong, they all knew that they needed to.

When we build walls because of hurts in our lives, they end up hurting us more than the one they were intended for. It eventually ensnares everyone who comes near us. God's word says, "When you stand praying, if you hold anything against anyone, forgive them, so that your Father in heaven may forgive you your sins."

Judgment Day is a day on which we will all need mercy. On that day, if we say, "I could not forgive, because of the hurt that someone caused me", then God will say, "I cannot forgive you your sins". Ouch!

I don't know about you, but on that day I need mercy. No matter how hard it is to forgive here on earth, I have to! The Bible says to forgive men when they sin against you, love those that hate you, and pray for those that use you. There is GREAT power in forgiving someone who does not deserve it! I know that this makes no sense to the human mind, but it is very true. It breaks down walls by crushing stones with invisible hammers.

Jean had a powerful encounter with this very thing. She had met a woman named Candy with whom she became close friends. Unbeknownst to Jean, Candy was an adulterer and was out to steal her husband. They had both attended the same church together, so it did not appear that any undermining was happening. Candy tried for weeks to seduce Jean's husband while she was unaware of her presence, but the smell of perfume was thick in the air behind her. Once Jean was made aware of the intentions of this adulterous woman, the feelings of betrayal and distrust filled Jeans thoughts. These feelings started to eat at her with an intensity that you could cut with a knife. Any time this woman's name came up, she would cringe in utter disgust. If she saw her at church or in the store, Jean would run the other way. Jean recognized that she could not go on like this; it was killing her inside, because she could not even look at the woman without hate.

One day the pastor gave a sermon on forgiveness, and Jean was extremely convicted by the Holy Spirit about the feelings she was having. She saw the woman across the church and, felt compelled by the spirit of God to go to her. When Jean reached her she wrestled with her feelings to hit this woman, as she felt she deserved it. Out of nowhere, Jean grabbed Candy and gave her a hug. Candy was caught so off guard, she did not know how to respond. Jean leaned toward her ear and whispered, "I forgive you" and with that Jean kissed Candy on the side of her cheek. Right then, Jean said she heard a sound like glass breaking over her and hitting the floor. Then she felt a huge weight fall off of her shoulders. Freedom!

Forgiveness releases us from bondage. The other party is never affected by our hatred; we are the one who gets bound up, or ends up getting sick. Hatred even opens the door to unwanted visitors.

I have taught drama at church and I am reminded of a skit that I did once. In the skit, I sat on a stool and prayed with passion, "Oh God, please use me to reach and help people everywhere I go, Amen!" At once the Lord showed up and started massaging my shoulders. I liked that, and expressed my pleasure with sounds appealing to my feelings. "Aaaah!" But all of a sudden, the Lord hit a spot on my shoulder that hurt. I about came off the stool, "Hold up," I said, getting off the stool, "Lord, that pain is fresh! Be gentle, I got that hurt when a friend of mine hung up on me, and for no good reason." I then added firmly, "That's the last time I talk to them!" I started feeling confident, but then looking over my shoulder I saw the Lord was asking me to sit back down on the stool; he needed to massage some more areas.

Enjoying the process, once again with glee, ohhh yeah, but then I came off the stool like lightning and yelled, "Ouch! Not there Lord, now that's really tender! That's an older injury from where I built a fence around the yard. I used bricks! Yep, a shovel and some good old red mason bricks! I used them to keep those pesky neighbors from coming over and trampling down my freshly planted flowers. Also, they constantly want to borrow things of mine. Why don't they just get a job, that way they can buy their own things, instead of always using mine? So, I took care of that, Lord. I built the fence to keep them OUT!" So be easy on that area, ok?" Looking over at the Lord, I saw that once again he wanted me to sit down for some more massaging. "Really?"

My back and shoulders were loaded with pain, from all kinds of things that I did to people to keep them out of my life. I wanted of course, to be used by God to help others, but how could I? I was in so much pain that I complained about it in detail, and to whoever would listen! Seeing the Lord motioning to me to sit once again, I relented. I humbled myself under the great therapist's hands. It was really needed. I sat down on the stool and said, "Okay Lord, go deep, whatever it takes! I just want to be used." With that said I saw him pull out a chisel from his tools and then heard a sound like the breaking of glass. I screamed in agony, OUUCHHHHHH!

Each person in the Bible study shared about how they had been hurt so deeply by someone in their lives. Then we had a time where we broke away in private to pray to God on our own. It was here that one particular lady started to cry in a corner of the room. I did not think anything was wrong until it got louder and louder and then she began to wail and I mean WAIL! Jean and I just looked at each other because something was just not right about her crying. We both pulled Reba aside and said, "Reba, we feel that there is a demon crying through this woman's hurt." We had discerned this, through the power of the Holy Spirit by the nature of her screaming. No one else in the room was aware of anything out of the ordinary that was going on. This was the work of the Holy Spirit who gave us the Word of Knowledge.

We thought that we were there on the island to evangelize in the streets, but God had a very different plan for us. Reba went to the woman screaming and asked her if we could pray with her the next morning. She agreed, and so.... we had another one to put on the list of deliverance. Yikes, they were adding up!

4 - The Battle

Remember the four sisters back in chapter one? Well, three of the four girls went over to the pastor's house where we were staying. Carla, the oldest sister, was out of town, so she could not be apart. Everyone had taken seats in the courtyard outside. Anne, Jean, Reba, Ricky and I all went outside to the courtyard to join them. Lynn and Marie were conveniently tired and had gone to bed early. We later found them hiding behind a curtain observing the whole drama. In the courtyard the girls started to share their stories of what was going on inside of them. They once again told us the story about living with their aunt and how she gave them Dwarf and Troll spirit guides. These spirits were to follow them throughout their lives. When I asked, "Did they see them?" They responded by saying, "Yes, they follow us everywhere." None of the girls could smile at us and Lisa seemed very depressed.

They told us that these spirits would show themselves at night in their homes and then follow them to their work places during the day. All of these girls had given their hearts to Christ about a year before but they were still under some type of curse. The pastors wanted us to see what we could do to get rid of these evil things.

Seriously? Ok! I started asking each one questions like "Do you talk to them?" "Yes", Lila replied, and added "I am in sin!" with that said, Lila stiffened her body, and her eyes were at a fixed stare straight ahead. Then slowly she reached out and tried to grasp at the Bible in my hand. We quickly started to command the spirits to let her go when she started choking! We all gathered around her to try and stop the demon from gagging her. Simultaneously, her sister Lisa started choking in her chair and Jenny, her other sister, started to rock back and forth.

The pastors and all of us just looked at each other; we had never seen anything like this before! Well I say that, but what they play at the movies and on TV these days is right on target to what was happening here. We took our positions and all started commanding the devils to let go of these girls and come out of them. Just then two of the ladies doubled over and started throwing up! Say What?

They were mimicking one another. When one would do something, the other sister would do the same thing. None of the girls were able to breath and they were barley coherent. We were trying desperately to keep them from passing out. We just kept saying the powerful name of Jesus Christ, the mighty deliverer! This was totally wide open crazy, in every way! The demons had them by the throat; there was no turning back now. Even though we did not understand it, we were not at all ready to shrink back. No we were in this thing full throttle, until the job was done!

We needed the anointing oil of the Holy Spirit to loosen the grip the enemy had over them. Something had a hold on them and was not letting go without a serious fight. We have found that some demons will not leave the home in which they have been resident in for years. That is not without a drag down fight; because they have been given a legal right to be there by the owner.

When we find a defiant fight like this, we must question the owner of the house to relinquish all squatter's rights, by asking them to repent from what allowed a spirit to access them. Although they initially had asked God to forgive them of all of their sins, these particular sins had to be renounced because they involved a covenant with the dark side. We have found that any involvement with the occult such as séances, Ouija boards, mediums, palm readers, Horoscope, Tarot cards, Wicca, pacts made with the devil, Dungeons and Dragons, spells, crystals etc.. It has to be broken. Renouncing it loosens the devils grip over the person and breaks the contract of evil that the enemy gained over them. When we ask God to forgive us of sin, he sends light to root out the darkness. Angels actually assist in the fighting, by pulling out the demon spirits.

After about two hours of intense battle for these three, Jean said she literally froze as she watched as Lisa threw back her head and saw a black spirit come up out of her mouth. Instantly, ALL of the ladies were delivered! Wow! ...They were all very exhausted, and said afterwards that they felt extremely light. They said they felt as if a big weight had been lifted off their shoulders.

We then had a tremendous time of dancing and celebration to Jesus Christ! I have never in my life seen such a transformation. The change on them was like night and day. You could not wipe the smiles off their faces, and all depression had left them! Thank you Father God! Incredible!

Here is one more incredible story of Great Joy.

I remember the time we were introduced to a teenage girl whose name was Joy. When we met her, we noticed that this beautiful girl could not smile, for her entire countenance had been stolen by the enemy. She lived in the deepest darkest depression I have ever seen before, for her face did not match her precious name of Joy.

We had been asked by her parents to come to their house to see if we might be able to help their daughter. When we arrived we could hear a massive loud noise. It sounded like wild animals were tearing apart their prey in the woods behind her house. A little nervous, I asked "What is that noise?" Her relatives responded, "Wild boar, they are in the woods, they travel in packs." I could not believe it! All I could think of was the story in the Bible about the pigs.

I kept thinking about this episode of the Gadarene in the book of Matthew: "No one could bind him, not even with chains, because he had often been bound with shackles and chains. When he saw Jesus from afar, he ran and worshiped Him. And he cried out with a loud voice and said, "What have I to do with You, Jesus, Son of the Most High God?" They kept begging Jesus earnestly that He would not send them out of the country. Now a large herd of swine was feeding there near the mountains. All the demons begged Him, saying, "Send us to the swine, that we may enter them." And at once Jesus gave them permission. Then the unclean spirits went out and entered the swine (there were about two thousand); and the herd ran violently down the steep place into the sea, and drowned in the sea"

Thoughts were flooding my mind; I realized then that we were walking the pages right out of the Bible! We had cast out the devil that had taken her smile that day. She revealed to us a full set of pearly whites as God's mighty light came to dispel the darkness that was in her. She was totally set free from the depression that kept her in prison. As for the boar in the woods, all I know is we never heard them again, once we started to pray. A--mazing!

5 - Shame

The society on the island is extremely poor. Each one of them has a little store in front of their home to try to bring in some type of revenue. Izabal is the name of the lady I described previously wailing in chapter three. She had been attending the church for years with her family and is an excellent seamstress. Because of her family's tremendous need for income, we all decided to buy her a sewing machine to start a business. We knew that the entire family would benefit from the business. Izabal and her daughter could sew, while Frank and the other children could promote sales with flyers. Because of the serious poverty on this Island, we had to have it delivered at night, because of horrible jealousy problems amongst the neighbors. I know that sounds crazy but it is a very sad fact. We did not want anyone to be mad at this family so we brought the whole family over to the pastor's house for the great reveal.

Before we presented the sewing machine we wanted to pray over them for blessing and prosperity. Just before we prayed I asked Izabal about the deep hurt that we had heard coming from her on Sunday night. She started to wail once again just like she had at the pastor's house that night in prayer. I asked her to look up at my eyes, because our eyes are the windows of the soul. Once she looked up, we saw it: a demon staring right back at us through Izabal's eyes.

Here we go again! Our team was stunned, to say the least, but ready for whatever the day had for us. Poor Izabal: this thing inside her bent her head down, making her feel absolutely shameful. She was wailing from deep rooted hurt from things done to her in her past. She could not raise her head on her own; it snickered at us and then threw her head down again in shame. Out of Izabal's mouth came a voice other than her own. "I am shaaame!" It growled. Shame always makes people feel like hiding under a rock.

We then started taking authority over this demon, yelling in the name of Jesus. Come out of her! All of a sudden it changed faces and mumbled in a low tone "I am rejection" Izabal on the other hand started crying so profusely and had no control over her own voice.

We used the Bible as a Sword, because that's what Gods Word says it is! Demon spirits know what this book, the Bible is, and when it is used as a Sword they are petrified! Now isn't that something? How many of us have these books just gathering dust in our houses? Demons believe and tremble in fear, but we barely know where ours is half the time, and never take it out of its sheath. No wonder we feel so defeated!

I once had a roommate who was having an affair with a married man. She went to church but somehow convinced herself that it was okay to do this and still worship God uninhibited. She was praying desperately to marry the man she was having the affair with but to no avail. However her prayers were hindered from being answered, because of the cloud of dust between her and God.

Her vision was impaired in both the natural and spiritual realms. Most of the time she wore contacts for she could not see at all without them, but when her eyes got really tired she would switch to her glasses. On occasion she would forget to take her contacts out before going to bed.

One night while she was sleeping I began to pray, and felt a deep burden for what she was doing. A lot of times, when I pray I open the Bible in front of me that I may hear His voice more clearly. My eyes fell on the scripture in Hebrews 4, it says "For the word of God is alive and active, sharper than any double-edged sword, it penetrates even to dividing soul and spirit, joints and marrow; it judges the thoughts and attitudes of the heart."

Well, being the dramatic person that I am, with my eyes I saw a book in my hand, but in the spirit realm this book was a SWORD!

That was all I needed. I got up and slowly crept toward her room. I carefully pushed her door open and looked to see if she was completely asleep. When I saw that the coast was clear I lifted my book high up toward the ceiling and brought it down in a striking sword stroke through the air. I yelled out in a whisper, "I use this mighty sword of God and divide your soul from your spirit! I command you to hear the Word of the Lord. Soul, I separate you from the spirit! You will stop sinning against the Lord God! You will not have an affair any longer." I kept making thrusting actions through the air with my sword until I finally felt that I better get out of there, so I left and went to my own bedroom.

In the morning I rose first and saw her coming out of her room with a puzzled look on her face. She staggered across the floor as if she had been drinking. She spoke groggily while rubbing her eye. "This is so weird; I went to bed with my contact in and woke up to find it sliced in half. That has never happened before!" I looked up toward the ceiling as she stumbled into the bathroom and motioned to God with a heart filled with passionate whispers of gratitude "It worked! Whahoo! Thank you Lord!" Then I danced back into the kitchen.

Knowing what I know today, we all gathered around Izabal ready for a show down. Another demon spoke, this time it was very aggressive, it snarled at us, "You don't know what she has done." We usually shut a demon like this up by applying the sword to its throat, so I pressed the Bible against Izabal's neck. This made the demon shut up, in Jesus' name! Her children and husband were present and this blasted evil spirit was going to exploit her sins in front of all of them! Her children said, "Its ok, we know everything about mom." But did they?

The children, who were in their twenties, told us that every night at the dinner table since they could remember, Izabal would proclaim endlessly what her father had done to her when she was a child. She would mourn tearfully day after day as she relived the horrible memories.

Her father abused her with mental, physical and sexual abuse. She was hurt so deeply that she could not forgive what he had done

21

to her. He had since passed away, but in her, he was very much alive. Unfortunately this un-forgiveness is what kept her BOUND UP. This sickening enemy seized those horrible moments of abuse and tied her up to be a prisoner all her life. When she got married it was carried into that relationship and also down to her children. She had no idea that anything had taken residence inside of her. Not realizing anything was wrong with her she slowly started to participate in sexual sins of all kinds because of what was done to her.

Ricky led her in a powerful prayer of forgiveness for her father, and then he had her bless her father. Even though he was dead, this was not for him, but for her freedom. This is very powerful to the unseen world; they thought that they had her for life, but they were wrong, they had her bound only until Jesus showed up.

Remember the service on forgiveness? This is what stimulated the Holy Spirit to target this precious woman of God and set her free of her afflictions.

Un-forgiveness is a very powerful way that the enemy can gain access into our lives, and it is not a pretty picture. Her father had molested her endlessly, so she hated him for it, not realizing that this hatred then turned inward to men in general. Hatred does not harm the person that did the hurt, it harms us that holds on to it.

It is like a serious deep cut in our flesh. If we leave it to heal on its own by ignoring it, infection starts to grow. Then any time the incident or person is mentioned, the hurt manifests all over again, spewing poisonous puss everywhere. If it is left in that state, it will eventually go to the heart. This is how our enemy works against us. Like an infection, he comes from the invisible to cause us pain, steal our peace and ruin our relationships. Then ultimately he goes in for the kill.

After leading her through this prayer the evil spirit lost its grip and came out of her with a long yawn. She looked free, but I cautiously studied her eyes to see if anything else was there. Izabal grabbed the top of my arm and ran her hand down it in a very lustful way, saying," Mmm I Looove youuuuuuuu." I turned and looked at her, and there it was: a new demon had come up in her eyes.

It was so defiant and again started snickering and mocking! Oh boy, a demon started confessing with force all the sexual acts that she had performed. This terrible creature was naming the different women and men that she had been with sexually, as recently as the week prior. Now, Izabal had been married for more than twenty years, and at that point we had no idea whether her husband and children knew any of this. The demon was so very seductive acting as it named all its victims. It was seething in delight as it hissed like a snake. It brought to mind the great prostitute mentioned in Revelations 17, she is staggering drunk on men's blood, she gloats that she has taken down the kings of the earth and utters blasphemies against God.

Here is a key to remember: demons hate us! They love to see us ruined. They come to steal everything we have. They destroy all our relationships, and make us so sick that we die, or make us so disgusted with ourselves that we take our own lives. They come to kill us!

We are all in this thing called LIFE together, to help one another, not to exploit each other. The Bible says in Romans 3:23, "We have all sinned and fallen short of God's glory!"

Once again we took our positions as warriors and started casting out these evil foul spirits by sending them to the pit of hell from where they came. The fight was fierce, but Jesus! Demons shriek at the Name of Jesus, His mighty powerful name! That is why men try to remove his image and name from our money, schools, courts etc., but it is not men doing it. No, it's a master spirit of Anti-Christ who uses men to do its will.

We also have mighty powerful angels that help us. I thank God that during the battle before the earth was formed, only one third of the angels turned evil. The other two thirds are with us.

Izabal's sinful behavior was a direct response to her abuse. It made her feel rejected, unloved, and she despised men inwardly because of what a man had done to her. These demons of sin had not only affected her, but her whole family. We saw so many of these particular spirits that it was uncanny. The men on this island would go to other nations to find work, because of poverty, leaving their women and children behind for years at a time. It became a woman driven society, leaving a huge door open for promiscuity and sexual affairs. It also promoted same sex relationships nationwide. Izabal was completely shameful of her actions, and this is what came out of her: the spirit of Shame, Rejection, Jealousy, Self-hatred, Sexual perversion and of course Un- forgiveness. It was insane!

I loved the way her husband and children gathered around her with their support and together cried buckets of healing tears. Finally the battle ended! Izabal was exhausted, but delivered! We praised our GOD with the highest praise our voices could give. What a great victory!

6 - The Machine

Ok, glad that's over with! When we took the family into the house to present the sewing machine to them, we noticed a situation.

We were getting ready to present Izabal with a sewing machine, because we wanted to provide a way to start a new business. Izabal is an incredible seamstress so this seemed like a great plan. We had all pooled our monies together so that we could get a top notch machine for them. We knew that Izabal's whole family would all be able to work this new family business. We also knew that this was going to bless their socks off, and now that Izabal was totally delivered, we could not wait for the great reveal!

We brought them all into the house and all stood in great anticipation in front of the sheeted machine. Frank said "Wow, what is this?" and tried to take a peek by lifting an edge of the sheet. The room was filled with electricity, as every eye was on the sheet, cameras ready. Here we go! Ricky removed the sheet! Izabal saw the corner of the machine as it was lifted; she jumped in the air and twirled wildly about, screaming through tears! Then the whole sheet came off to reveal a beautifully polished Singer sewing machine. This brought them to their knees in humble adoration for us and God for blessing them so abundantly. We prayed once again, thanked God and then watched with great joy as they took a heavenly bath! Everyone was crying through great joy, everyone that is except Todd their son.

As we were praying I opened my eyes to see Todd backing up from the group. I hit Anne and Jean's arm and brought them over to the pastor's wife and said, "Watch Todd." He made his way to a corner of the room and looked as if he was going into a deep depression. We watched closely as the family on the left danced with glee, and Todd their son regressed into the darkness. His whole demeanor was sinking in sorrow.

I walked over to him and said, "Todd take my hand, what's wrong?" Todd could not even look at me. I asked him if he would like prayer? He nodded his head yes so I led him by the hand to our sanctuary out in the courtyard. I was thinking as we were walking out there, if his reaction could be because of everything his mother had said in her deliverance. After all, the children knew everything that had been done to her, but they knew nothing at all of the "sins" she had been committing. been committing. I thought maybe, all he needs is some counseling or something like that. Oh boy was I wrong! The celebration came to a halt, as poisonous snakes of all kinds were slowly slithering in from all directions around us.

I am reminded of a story that may give you a clearer picture of what was going on here. One day a friend of mind came to me in embarrassment about their bathroom. They told me the mold and mildew was out of control. I told them that I could take a look but was not sure if I could tackle it on my own. It was a huge bathroom, but I took the challenge, and my friend Anne and I showed up at the house to clean the bathroom. The shower was FULL of mold and still growing more! If only they would have cleaned it on a regular basis, this would not have happened! Bleach is a really good idea!

We had been there for what seemed an eternity, but to our amazement all the mold came up, scrubbed away. Anne and I stood with smiles on our faces in victory over the monster of mildew. Oh, the Glory of it all! We felt great, but then came time to rinse it all down the drain. Then I turned on the shower to try to thoroughly rinse. I was using a cup to splash water on all sides of the tiles that the flow of water could not reach. When I hit the back of the tiled wall the mold started coming out of the seams of the grout. It was coming out in clumps onto the shower floor, I could not believe it!

I rinsed and rinsed but the mold had grown up into the walls and now it had been forced by the bleach to loosen its grip. Anne and I spent forty-five minutes aggressively rinsing and rinsing, as it would not stop coming out of the grout. Finally, through blood, sweat and tears the job was complete, and the bathroom was a dream! I hope this helps describe what was happening here on this island. The job was huge and exhausting, but God gave us strength and enabled us to conquer the diseased mold problem.

As I write this book, I can clearly see when I look at what a courtyard or courthouse represents. It is a place where laws are established and judgment is placed on one who breaks the laws set in place. I think it's incredibly interesting how God also orchestrates the settings of things on this island in a similar fashion.

Before I fully go into what transpired with Todd I must back up just a tad, and tell you a little about Todd and his sister CeeCee. Everywhere in the world there are customs that are passed down from generation to generation. One of them is that, when parents get older, and they can't work or get sick, they force their children to take on a huge burden by working the rest of their lives to provide for them. The elder children have to find a job, lay their lives aside and toil and spin in the job market to provide for their sick, disabled mom and dad and often many kids.

This puts a huge burden on the children and causes stress, anxiety and depression. CeeCee, who is the eldest child, was forced to quit the ministry that she loved, to care for her mom, dad and five siblings. Her desire was to work with children through, teaching and counseling, but she would never see that dream happen. She struggled terribly to make enough money, to care for all six family members. Todd was next in line to take on the burden of finding a job, so that he could help relieve the pressure put on CeeCee. Todd and CeeCee were just out of their teenage years, and were extremely stressed that they would never be able to fulfill their dreams, because of this huge burden.

Jesus talks about this kind of burden in Matthew 9:59 "He said to a man "Follow me." But he replied, "Lord, first let me go and bury my father." Still another said, "I will follow you, Lord; but first let me go back and say goodbye to my family." Jesus replied, "No one who puts a hand to the plow and looks back is fit for service in the kingdom of God." "What does this mean?" Does he not care about our loved ones? Yes, he does! He encourages us all throughout the Bible, to do good, to love our neighbor, and help the poor. He also says, "Take my burden, it's easy and light! And do not let men burden you down with heavy loads." He is all about LOVE, not burdens! He tells us to lay down our lives, not to men but to Him, there is a difference. God does desire for us to care for the elderly and orphans, but He does not want it to cloud our view for seeking Him first.

Todd and his sister came crying to us in secret, because of fear of their mom and dad, to discuss their situation. As they lay their heavy burden on the kitchen floor, we turned to God's Word. We found that God's desire is for CeeCee's mom and dad (Izabal and Frank) to fully rely on Him, not their children. He is very able to answer their prayers, and free their children from slavery. The reason that they don't pray is because it is very hard work! Most of the time it does not come easy, but when it comes, it is rewarded with gold, like faith. A lot of times we choose the Ishmael way instead of the Isaac way.

When they heard this Word, we saw an incredible happening; something like scales fell from their eyes! They both saw how this weight on their shoulders was just an island custom. They had taken on the island's customs, not God's Word! Once they realized they were actually children of God, not children of customs, the burden melted into the air.

7 - Chains Vanish

Todd and CeeCee now had the keys to unlock the chains that had been put on their feet. Both were dancing, knowing that our God was going to answer their prayers! I could hear the song playing: "Loose, Footloose, kick off your Sunday shoes! Lose, your blues, everybody go footloose!" Oh what a victory they felt! But now, how to break the news to mom and dad?

The whole family was in awe when they removed the cover that was on the sewing machine, everyone except Todd that is. He was now sinking quickly into quick sand. His only hope was for Christ to throw him down a rope! I had led him by the hand back to the courtyard, because it had now become our church, and Todd was in the hot seat. Poor baby, he looked a wreck! I said, "Todd what is happening to you?" He said, "I'm in sin, I have had ungodly relationships with men." Then he started to slump in his chair in absolute despair. He hung his head in shame, he could not look up, because shame had held his head so low it almost touched the chair he sat in. When I heard him say that he was in a homosexual relationship like his mom was. I knew that this was the same evil spirit that had attacked her. This evil spirit in Todd now was provoked to raise its ugly head up, when it heard its name called only minutes earlier with Izabal. Once it heard its name mentioned in Izabal, it manifested in Todd as well, because it was agitated and woke up within him. This awakening happened because of the anointing of Christ's presence and authority in the courtyard. It had no alternative but to submit under Christ's lordship.

I was so angry with this enemy, because he dangles sin in our faces like a delicious red apple and entices us by our own lusts to sin. With seduction on his lips He slowly says, "Go ahead and pick it up, smell it, doesn't it smell good? Now close your eyes and dream, yes, dream of what it would be like to just taste it. Twirling it in your mouth, mmm is it not good? Don't you want it? You can have it, just look at its color. Oh it is so good to the eye, isn't it? Now BITE IT!"

If we listen to his voice long enough, we will eventually bite and then eat the bait. Once we eat it, he traps us by our own desires; it turns black in our mouth and then poisons our body. The Bible tells us in James 1:14-15, "Each person is tempted when they are dragged away by their own evil desire and enticed. Then, after desire has conceived, it gives birth to sin; and sin, when it is full-grown, gives birth to death." Don't be deceived!

Todd opened wide the door and the devil freely came in. All he wanted was companions to like him, but in his quest for friends it turned sexually perverted. The devil came in like a flood and we needed to get him out. Todd confessed his sin, and now that the enemy was found out, it could hide no longer. However, when we tried to cast it out, it would not budge! It had dug into him, like a tick sucking his blood! A tick hangs on until it is pried away from its victim. We bound up, tied up, loosed, cast down, yelled and took authority with great force until we became hoarse, but it would not move from its position.

Now the very cool thing is, every morning we would get up and have a powerful prayer time together, and then throughout the day God would use us in His powerful gifts of the spirit. I love this! While we were praying for Todd I noticed through the gate of the courtyard there were peering eyes staring back at us. We were making a lot of noise out in the courtyard, but people in the neighborhood also knew this was the pastor's house and noise was inevitable on a daily basis. This however was different, oh yes it was, when you're in the middle of an exorcism, things out of the ordinary just happen. We watched as the eyes would disappear then reappear. Then I looked at Todd, who was melting in the chair under a spell. Finally Cary, a guy from the church came out from the dark and revealed himself. When my eyes met Cary's, The Holy Spirit said to me through a word of knowledge. "Pull Cary in the courtyard, because he is the strong-man." I said, "Seriously Lord, what if he does not come?"

What I mean by "strong man" is not what some may be thinking. Not a strong man, but rather THE STONG MAN. In Matthew 12:28 it says "If I cast out demons by the Spirit of God, surely the kingdom of God has come upon you. How can one enter a strong man's house and plunder his goods, unless he first binds the STRONG MAN? Then he will plunder his house." Cary was in a sense the Leader of the pack, a PACK of demons that is!

Knowing this by the Holy Spirit I yelled, "Hey Cary, can you come in the courtyard?" With that said he opened the gate and slowly came forward to where we were standing. I then asked him if he would not mind taking a seat. The state of Todd at that moment had gotten worse when Todd saw Cary, because he was paralyzed and in a trance. Right now all of our attention was on Cary, knowing that the Holy Spirit had just said he was the strongman and Todd was under his authority somehow. As for Cary, he was in for the ride of his life or maybe should I say we were. I started asking Cary a few casual questions, when suddenly he started shaking and his eyes rolled back in his head. We all looked at each other and I thought, "Wow, now the battle begins! Yikes!

8 - Strongman Spirit

Cary was squirming and grabbing with intensity to his chair, just clinging to it like his nerves were unraveling within him. In other words, we (or, rather, angels) were binding him up with God's ropes. He rocked back and forth and was moving his head around and around as if he had autism. Hmmm, it sure looked like a "Life Time" movie in the making, for sure!

Somehow in the heat of the moment we lost contact with Todd, who sat motionless in his chair. We saw very clearly that Cary was Todd's problem. We first had to cast out the strong man spirit controlling Cary before the demon in Todd would come out. When Cary cocked his head back, he would catch Todd's eyes then Todd would come alive, and buckle up like an abused animal. Todd seemed to be fully controlled by Cary. Whatever was going on in Todd was subject to the higher hierarchy that was in Cary. It was wild to say the least! This was similar to the girls that were delivered previously because all of them were connected together too! The more dominate one in the group seemed to rule the others; it's just like an army ranking system. Little did we know that the atmosphere around us was heating up to a boiling point?

In our world as we know it, we have armies with corporals and generals and privates. In the spirit world that we cannot see, they also have armies, where one is subject to another. We read about hierarchies or kings and princes of such armies in the Bible. Something like this is recounted in Daniel, when a mighty angel is fighting a strong man or demon spirit over the geographical area of Persia. Michael, a warrior angel over God's people is called to help the first angel to get to Daniel to tell him his prayer has been heard. In that passage of scripture where God is speaking to Daniel it says "Then he said to me, "Do not fear, Daniel, for from the first day that you set your heart to understand, and to humble yourself before your God, your words were heard; and I have come because of your words. But the prince of the kingdom of Persia withstood me twenty-one days; A Demonic Prince over that area, Michael, a mighty Angel of God one of the chief princes of God, came to help me, for I had been left alone there with the kings of Persia, a demonic force." Dan 10:1-6 (NKJ).

I try and stay away from science fiction movies about ghost, witches or exorcisms because they scare me. The problem is I know that these things are a reality. Others can go to them with no reservations because they believe that these things are just not real. We live in world of faith that we can just step into. How amazing it is to be a part of it?

Back to the sanctuary, things were really steaming up in Cary, because a very strong spirit was manifesting. Cary was not able to talk, because this thing had his throat and was choking him. We were all trying to prevent this from happening by holding his head back while fighting this beast. Every time he would try to speak, Todd would curl up his nose at him, and hiss like a snake. Seriously? Just when things could not get any worse, we heard the rusty courtyard gate creak open. We all looked up to see who or what it was, and then we were completely blown away.

9 - Mummies

In came Coco one of the head mediums of the Spiritist church in that area. It was very eerie, for it was after midnight with a full moon lightning up the sky, if you know what I mean. I could not believe it! She just opened the gate, grabbed a chair came up to Cary and just stared at him, without saying a word. Then Coco's sister and several others came one by one through the gate. They all grabbed patio chairs without speaking a word. There was a fixed glare on each of their faces, as each one seemed to be on a mission. They never looked up, but pulled up their chairs six inches from Cary to stare at him. Cary, who was very seductively rubbing his body with his hands, cocked his head over at them and smiled sheepishly. Have you ever seen the movie Mummies? Well, here we were, in real life time! Todd on the other hand, sat like a wounded child cowering in a corner with his thumb in his mouth.

What! You have got to be kidding me? All the deliverances that we were doing just then came to an abrupt halt! Stop the press! We all looked at each other and instantly knew what was going on. We could not believe this was happening, we were in TOTAL amazement! Anne and I looked at each other and she said, "Are you serious? We can't do deliverance on Cary! There is a major demonic fortress being formed here." Then pointing she said, "And all of these mummy-like people have the same familiar spirit." I said, "Ah yeah!" We turned to look at the pastors; they knew what was happening as well, and they made a move on it. Thank God, they started making everyone leave. It was the weirdest thing I have ever seen in this life. They spoke not a word as the pastor and his wife said, "Come on, you must leave." They were all in a trance-like state, like mummies coming out of a graveyard, and they all walked out of the gate just as freaky as they had come in. This was out of the crypt, very strange! It reminds me of this verse found in Numbers 23:24 "The people rise like a lioness; they rouse themselves like a lion that does not rest till it devours its prey and drinks the blood of its victims." Time for an Excedrin!

"The people rise like a lioness; they rouse themselves like a lion that does not rest till it devours its prey and drinks the blood of its victims." Numbers 23:24

10 – The Courtyard

I had to pinch myself to see if I was dreaming this whole thing or not, was it surreal, or SO real! We had all realized that these people had come into the courtyard to give Cary, or the demons in him, a power punch. The demonic grip was growing very weak inside of Cary and Todd. We were gaining victory, and Satan knew it, so he brought in reinforcements. They were refueling Cary like a gas station fill up. Though one may be overpowered, two can defend themselves. A cord of three strands is not easily broken. Although we had authority in Jesus Christ, we had no idea of what was actually happening in the air above us. We had just walked into a hornet's nest and I must say I hate those insects, because they sting. What would retaliation look like?

These spirits were very strong and territorial. An extremely dominant perversion and sexual spirit was in control of the whole city. These things were not going down without a serious fight. They were strategizing and re-planning on how to sabotage God's plan.

We could see one still lagging behind, peering through the steel bars, not willing to leave all the way. It looked like their refueling power punch had worked. Todd looked as if he was being pulled slowly out of the quicksand he had previously been sinking in. Cary grabbed the air in from of him and lunging forward, he cocked his head back over my way.

He then looked straight at me and whimpering, he slurred, "Renee, whyyyy are you so mad at me?" When I looked at him eye to eye, he raised his upper lip and growled like a mad dog. I sighed deep and grunted, "Really?" With that, a spirit came off of Cary and hit me so hard I did not know who I was! I backed up, and shook my head as if I'd been knocked out cold. I turned the opposite direction and headed toward the house. "Okay" I said, "I don't know what just happened but I'm out of here."

Anne saw what had just happened and stopped me, saying "Renee, what is wrong with you? And where are you going?" I said, "Girl, I'm done here, someone else needs to take over, something has happened to me, I quit!" She said, "What? You can't quit, we are in the middle of a huge deliverance!" I said, "Yes I know, sorry, but I'm done! Bye-bye. " Then Jean grabbed me and said, "Renee, what is wrong? What is happening to you?" I said, "Fear has just made my head spin, then it jumped on my back, and knocked me to the ground. I am engulfed in some type of black soot, now I need prayer!" Then I headed for the house. Jean and Anne told Cary and Todd they could go home. They both looked at each other in amazement, as if they had been set free from prison, actually they had!

Needless to say, the place was now in absolute turmoil! Todd was in a fog and Cary slowly got up like an energizer bunny with low batteries. He saw me walking away, and said, groping for his words, "Renee, can I talk to you?" I looked back, and thought I was going to black out. I turned to meet him half way when he said, "Renee I am in sin really bad." I said, "I know Cary, do you feel anything happening in you?" He then nodded his head in agreement. I said, "Do you want to be set free?" He said, "Yes I do, can you help me?" I said, "Yes, but not tonight." With that, he opened the gate and he and Todd staggered like drunks down the street. As for me, I needed my mommy. I turned to our group and said, "I need prayer, and a deep shoulder massage would help too."

11 ~ Reloading Ammunition

Oh yes, I needed serious prayer! I felt as if I had a black eye, and I had not seen that coming! My sweet sisters had my back and bathed me in a flood of prayers. The enemy thought that he had the upper hand because he had dealt such a hard blow. But just like in a wrestling match when your opponent has you pinned down, the referee will blow the whistle and break you apart. That is what my sisters did for me, through prayer. This prayer was so needed: we needed to reload our ammunition, believe me, because this was no ordinary battle! I had no idea how big this opponent actually was.

Have you heard of David and Goliath? Goliath appeared to be huge and David was just a very small boy. I was out one morning with my dog walking in the cool of the morning. I was praying for needs that I had with intense passion. When I turned around to go back home I saw my shadow. I was blown away because it was huge! I was in awe over the size of it, so I snapped a picture on my cell phone to remind me at how the enemy views us when we pray.

Thank GOD that our enemy is invisible, because we just might have run away if we could see them. Wait a minute, I did! The Bible says we are in a wrestling match with the enemy. Wrestling is not for weaklings; it means upfront and personal contact. I don't know about you, but I don't want to see some scaly, slimy, sulfuric ruler of darkness, or hosts of wickedness. When I thrust my sword in the air, I just believe I am hitting my target square in the heart; I don't have to see it, we just have to believe, so we armored up.

That next day everyone went to the mall to rest, and shop of course, except for me and Anne. It was my turn once again to speak at the church. They had planned a service on Friday morning. The Pastor and his wife were calling it the HOLY SPIRIT conference. Ricky had pulled me aside and said, "Renee, we are going to the mall, you stay here and go to The Mountain of God, make sure you go to the Mountain!" Whatever that meant, I said, "Ok, I will!" What he really meant to say was, "Renee, while we are gone; study Gods word, and get a good message for us". I thought, "Mountain of God, Okay!", and with that, off they went to the mall.

I was thinking, "Yippy, I have a lot of free time!" I did study after they left, but my mind kept wandering. Can you relate? Anne and I talked and shared testimonies of our daily happenings and ate some goodies in the kitchen. I was feeling good, until the team returned from the mall. It seemed like only minutes had passed by, but they said it had been hours. I could not concentrate like I wanted to, but felt I had enough hot buttered bread to bring to the church table. I was confident that the message would be good if God showed up, that is! Ricky on the other hand said, "Renee did you go to the mountain?" I said, Uhhh... sure. "He looked directly at me, and repeated, "Renee did you go, to the MOUNTAIN?" I said, "I have a message on the Holy Spirit prepared if that is what you mean?" That's when Ricky came over, shook me and said, "DID YOU GO TO THE MOUNTAIN?"

I then said sheepishly, bahhh, bahhh, I'm just kidding. "Well, nn-ooo, not exactly, I don't think, I did." Ricky pleading with me again, saying, "Renee, you have to go, to the MOUNTAN OF GOD!" Now I was intimidated, and I'm not an easy person to intimidate. I was starting to feel pressure, I mean it's not like I am this great preaching machine or anything. I am confident about coming up with a message, but seriously now. What was he saying? What was this MOUNTAIN OF GOD he was talking about? Is there really such a place? If so, how do I find it? Ricky really wanted me to hear from God. I guess I had it all wrong. I had to get away by myself, put on my mountain shoes and start climbing. Did he know something that I didn't?

12 – Lions

"Where is the lions' den, that feeding place for young lions? Where are the lion, the lioness, and the lion cub that moved about with no one to terrify them? The lion tore its prey to pieces to feed its cubs. It strangled the prey for its mate. It used to fill its caves with torn carcasses and its dens with torn flesh. I am against those who are against me," declares the LORD of Armies. "A sword will kill your young lions. I will remove your prey from the earth, and no one will ever hear the voice of your messengers again." Nahum 2:11-12 (GWT)

The people on this Island are predominantly Catholic in their beliefs. Since I was born and raised Catholic, I felt confident that I knew what they believed in. However, many of the homes that we went into showed signs of a deep deterioration in their spiritual foundation. A lot of these Catholics had shrines set up in their homes, along with idols that they used as good luck symbols. I remember when I was young; I too had a good luck rabbit foot. I kept it with me where ever I went, and whenever something good happened to me, I attributed it to the magic rabbit foot. I also read my astrology report every day in the morning newspaper; in hopes that it would direct my path. If my day happened to turned out the way the astrology report said it would, then I would attribute astrology to having power.

Although I went to church, my belief system was built on a sinkhole. I had put my trust in other things besides God; therefore it left for a shaky foundation of my spiritual house. I did not read

God's word on how to live right, so I believed in whatever wave of doctrine that came my way and worked. I was trying to serve God, with an idol in my hand.

Since then, I gave my entire life over to Him and I have learned to follow His word for direction. I found this story in 1 Kings 17:2 that may shed some light on what I am saying. "Each national group made its own gods in the several towns where they settled. The people burned their children in the fire as sacrifices to these gods. They worshiped the Lord, but they also worshipped at the high places, they served their own gods in accordance with the customs of the nations from which they had been brought. The king of Assyria brought people from Babylon; he settled them in the towns too. When they first lived there, they did not worship the Lord; so lions came among them and they killed some people. It was reported to the king, the people you deported and resettled in the towns do not know what God requires. He has sent lions among them, which are killing them off, because the people do not know what He requires." Then the king of Assyria gave this order: "Have one of the priests go back to live there and teach the people what the God of the land requires." So one of the priests came to live in Bethel and taught them how to worship the Lord." Then the lions left.

That was what was happening on this island; they had gods of all kinds. No one knew who the real god was. The pastor did not preach on how to stay clean and live right, for fear that he would lose the people that came to his church if he preached too hard. The people that came to his church were not getting fed by God's word so they lived however they saw fit. He realized he needed to change his message, but it was too late. The people had already heaped sin upon themselves, making warm comfy homes for demonic spirits to live in.

We heard that several of them were having very scary dreams, or should I say nightmares. Teen agers were actually seeing ghost in the fields, not only at night, but in broad day light, while having their morning coffee.

In their search for answers, they went to church, but there they only said a canned prayer, sang a hymn, and had a touch of

Holy Water. The very place that should have helped them to get in touch with God came up empty and full of religion. What they were looking for was how to deal with their spiritual problems; as a result, like I said earlier, they filled their houses with shrines and idols. Hoping that touching them before they left for the day might ward off evil spirits.

He is not a religion, as some may think; He only desires to be worshiped by us; He desires for us to love him with our heart, mind and soul, not from a religious forum. When we give Him our lives, He comes into us and lives. He then gives us a desire to read His Word and then He begins to reveal Himself to us. In turn He speaks to us like a father speaks to his children or how a friend speaks to their friend.

We must pray in these days lying ahead of us as we never have prayed before. We must pray for wisdom and discernment to know the difference between light and darkness. You would think that the contrast is obvious, but that's not always so. The enemy of our souls slowly adds error into our lives, as if he is making a cake of evil. He stirs the contents of the mixing bowl, adding error along the way, until there is more error than batter. We can't see the difference because we have not taken the time to read God's directions for our lives as recorded in the Bible. Often the very book that can save our lives is found gathering dust on our bookshelves, so when error or deception filters in, we accept it with no restraints. This deception leaves us with a deep, thick film covering our eyes so that we can no longer see clearly. Now we need surgery, but getting the one who is deceived to realize this need is near impossible.

We informed them that God is only a conversation away. He is not afraid of evil or darkness, for He is a brilliant light and demons run from Him. It was imperative that they call out to the real god, but who was he? The five of us had come to share with them that Jesus was the God they needed. When they understood this relationship that God wanted with them, it made perfect sense, and they could not wait to give Him, their lives.

Once they believed, God forgave all their sins and made them His children, which gave them the right to have his authority and received power, not just any form of power, but His Mighty Power backing them up, to overcome *all* the evil of the enemy. This was GREAT news!

13 - Black Spirits

We were all in prayer in our big bedroom when there was a rustling at the bedroom door. Everyone in the house was in the room so it seemed quite weird that someone would want in. Marie got up to answer the door, but no one was there. Not thinking anything of it really, we continued to pray. In the heat of our prayers there it was again, a scuffling sound at the door. Again we opened the door to see who it was, but again no one was there. This time, however, a black presence slid into the room. "What was that?!" Anne shouted. I believe everyone saw it, because suddenly we all gasped. At once we took authority over whatever it was.

Ricky cleared his voice and started to share with us about the house. He said that before they had moved into the house it had been occupied by a warlock and witch doctor. He continued by saying that these guys would do séances and called up evil spirits to come live with them in the house. Reba then said, "Everyone who comes into this house has seen these spirits, because they reside in this particular bedroom!

Stunned, I shouted, "No way, in this bedroom?" Surely, this was not happening, I just knew I was dreaming. I pinched myself in hopes that I would wake up, and it would somehow all be a bad dream. When I looked around the room, everyone seemed so very serious. That's when I said, "Fine, then where is my blanky so I can hide? I'm Gone!" Now I know that sounds like a real spiritual Giant right? Look, I'm from an itty-bitty city in Pennsylvania; if we ever saw a black spirit go across the room, we called it a floater in our eyes. We were not used to all this evil spirit stuff our Christianity had moved to a different level. This island appeared to be living on the edge of Hates, for demons were manifesting left and right something we were not familiar with. The word "normal" had been removed from our vocabulary, because nothing and I mean nothing was by any means normal on this Island or in the days ahead of us.

I remember being at a youth camp as a little girl, camping out in the open forest in a tent. All of us would gather around the campfire at night. We would make s'mores and tell scary ghost stories. I held on to the girl next to me, listening with intensity, until someone shouted right in my ear, "BOO!" Needless to say the laps of the girls next to me became my home! I did not realize then how very real this invisible world is. God's Word says that when we encounter these things we should not be afraid of them, but should cast them out. I was trying to overcome this fear slowly, but seeing evil spirits there was an hourly experience, there was nothing slow about it. Just as soon as we had a moment to breathe in the dugout somewhere, BOOM, we were up to bat again! So I was forced to face my fear in a face to face combat!

We had our Swords drawn ready for battle! The Bible tells us in Mathew 15:13 that we are not to fight aimlessly like we are blind, but to become an expert swordsman by hitting our target square in the heart. This only comes by studying, reading and praying the Bible. The Bible became my very best friend, never leaving my side; it spoke as if it were a treasure map telling me what to do next. I am telling the truth! It was nothing short of AMAZING!

Reba had left for a minute, and then burst back into the room like a torpedo, searching behind curtains and inside cupboards. While thrashing my sword in the air (Bible) at high speeds and declaring Gods Word out loud I asked, "Reba what are you doing?" She said, "I just saw the black spirits come in here. This is where they hide, I'm looking for them." "Oh, okay, just wondering. That's all, thanks" I said timidly.

At that point Marie started to sing "What a Mighty God", and we all joined her. I sang but kept one eye open to the bedroom door, just in case "IT" decided to show itself. We sang until the presence of God came into the room, because we knew NO demon of hell could reside there.

In the Bible it says in Judges 7, "The Lord told Gideon to take the men to the river, "Separate those who cup the water with their hands and lap with their tongues from those who kneel down to drink." Three hundred of them drank from cupped hands, lapping like dogs. All the rest got down on their knees to drink. God was distinguishing between those who watched with an eye for the enemy, from those who drank on their knees and paid no attention to the enemy around them. So I was just keeping in sync.

We never saw the evil spirits manifest again, thank God! After all was calm, we cleaned our hands and purified our hearts, and then I stole away to a quiet place by myself. This is where I started my ascent up the mountain. I was as prepared as I could be. God says in His Word, "Who shall go up into the mountain of the Lord? Or stand in His Holy Place? It is He who has clean hands and a pure heart, which has not lifted himself up to what, is false or sworn deceitfully." Psalms 127

14 - The Mountain of God

Reba's kitchen was transformed into a motion picture. I had been studying in the Bible about Elisha and how he followed his mentor Elijah everywhere he went. I was pondering these scriptures for a while wondering how they might apply to the day of Pentecost in Acts 2, when the words on the page literally illuminated right in front of me. I was reading in *2 Kings 2:11 "When suddenly, a chariot of fire appeared with horses of fire, and separated the two of them; and Elijah went up by a whirlwind into heaven."*

That's when it happened; I was being sucked into the Bible just like The Chronicles of Narnia. The walls of the kitchen peeled back and in came a huge chariot of fire! Elisha was by the fire on one side and Elijah was going up into a whirlwind on the other side. All this was happening right in front of me. I could literally feel the mighty force of wind coming from the chariot. Elisha looked up and grabbed the anointed robe that Elijah just tossed to the ground. That's when the chariot took off and went sailing through the kitchen ceiling. I fell to the floor, and knew I had just seen Pentecost in a whole new way.

Acts 2:2 says, and suddenly there came a sound from heaven, as of a rushing mighty WIND, and it filled the whole house where they were sitting. Then there appeared to them divided tongues of FIRE, and one sat upon each of them. And they were all filled with the Holy Spirit and began to speak in a number of different languages as the Spirit prompted them.

2 Kings says there was fire, wind and a powerful anointing given to Elisha. I too had just seen an absolutely incredible demonstration of Pentecost in the kitchen on that morning!

After several hours went by, I tried to scramble myself up off the floor. I struggled to stand to my feet, because they kept going out from underneath me. Trying my best to stand, I grabbed on to the nearest wall for support, as my legs were like Jell-O. I attempted to go back into the bedroom to take a shower, but I was in no shape to stand in a puddle of water. I managed to prop myself up against the bedroom door, then I looked up at the ceiling from which the scene unfolded. I started to talk to God. I could barely mouth the words to him when I babbled out, "Lord, I under... stannnd... what it means tooooo... climbbb the m-m-m-ountain", and with that, I began to wail, because the presence of God was so very strong upon me. I had just been visited by the God of the universe, "The Great I am." Now, how was I going to explain this to the others?

15 - The Wind

It was five in the morning when I stumbled through the bedroom door, still under the influence of Gods power. There is no telling if I would even make it to the bathroom. Not thinking anyone was up yet, I met up with Anne, who was drying her hair in the hallway. She stopped the dryer and said, "How was your night?" I was trembling as I mumbled, "Uhhh... I went to the Mountain, and felt the w-w-wind...of God." I waved my hand in the air to explain the wind, and Anne fell to the floor sobbing. I was again doubled over in tears pouring my heart out to God. Anne was pinned to the floor and I was of no help to assist her. Of course, that stirred the other girls to wake as we just could not control our volume. Just then I poked my head up to see Jean who had risen from the dead of sleep, trying to get by us to use the bathroom, Yeah, good luck getting by us!

When Jean came close to us, she too fell to the floor and started wailing. By now Lynn and Marie were stirring in their beds to see what was happening, scared to get up. They just lay there in wonderment. When I fell into the doorway of their room, I said, "The Wind of God... is here." Just then Lynn was filled with the Holy Spirit, just like on the day of Pentecost in the Bible! She was speaking in languages that we had never ever heard before. Marie went to stand up and was knocked to the floor. She tried over and over but could not stand on her feet. If anyone off the streets came into the house right then, they would have thought we were all drunks. Does this sound familiar?

The Bible says in Acts 2:2 "When they heard the loud noise, everyone came running, and they were bewildered to hear their own languages being spoken by the believers. They were completely amazed. "How can this be?" they exclaimed. And we all hear these people speaking in our own languages about the wonderful things God has done!" They stood there amazed and perplexed. "What can this mean?" But others in the crowd ridiculed them, saying, "They're just drunk, that's all!" Then Peter stepped forward with the eleven other apostles and shouted to the crowd, "Listen carefully, all of you, fellow Jews and residents of Jerusalem! Make no mistake about this. These people are not drunk, as some of you are assuming. Nine o'clock in the morning is much too early for that."

I now know what Ricky meant when he shook me and said, "You have to GO TO THE MOUNTAIN!" Had he been to this Mountain? Did he go whenever he was to preach? Or was he prompted to tell me to "Go to the Mountain" by a higher authority? Whatever it was, or whoever it was, I would enquire later, I was just glad that I had gone! Now was the big moment, I needed to get the pastors up, but I didn't know how I would get to their room, as I could not move!

16 - Visions

Act 2:17 says "'in the last days, God says, I will pour out my Spirit on all people. Your sons and daughters will prophesy, your young men will see visions, your old men will dream dreams."

I managed to open our bedroom door, doubled over; I stumbled to the pastor's bedroom. They had not woken up yet. I wondered how anyone could sleep through all that noise. When I made it to their room I mumbled, "P-p-p-p-pastor, I w-w-w-went to the m-m-mountain, come," and I motioned with my hand the way. When we arrived in our room everyone was on the floor wailing for they could not get up. When Ricky and Reba walked into the room the wind of God hit them as well, and they too fell to the floor.

We couldn't make this kind of thing up even if we tried. There is no way a tiny little clay body can stand up to His mighty presence. When Jesus was in the garden, and the soldiers came to arrest him, Judas kissed Jesus to tell the soldiers who he was. When the soldiers asked Jesus, "Are you the Christ?" He replied "I AM" When Jesus said this, the soldiers all fell to the ground, because they could not stand when His Glory was revealed.

His presence was so very strong upon me that I once again got caught up in the Spirit of God and had another vision. The wall in the bedroom was peeled back and I was in the street. I saw multitudes of people coming out of their houses and the brightest light I have ever seen in my life (His Glory) was flooding the streets. Everyone had Bibles in their hands and all were heading to the church. At the church I saw the five of us ladies lay hands or just point and everyone there was healed instantly. Demons were flying out of people everywhere and everyone melted under the presence of God like butter to the floor. I then felt compelled to prophecy for I could hear a voice coming from my inner being; saying, "Nothing is impossible, nothing is impossible, nothing is impossible." Then I proclaimed boldly to the heavens, "Nothing is IMPOSSIBLE to those who believe!" As I spoke these words I was flipped upside down on the bed, uttering the mysteries of God with groans from deep inside of me.

In Romans 8 it says, "The Spirit himself intercedes for us through wordless groans. And he who searches our hearts knows the mind of the Spirit, because the Spirit intercedes for God's people in accordance with the will of God."

Paul's says that he was caught up in the spirit of God with visions. He says, "Whether in the in the body or out of the body I do not know." This is how I felt.

17 - The Cloud

I was totally caught up in the spirit of God when I lunged toward the bedroom door and said, "Let's go see!" I had no idea of what I was even doing; all I remember is in the Bible something similar happened.

Luke 9:28-36 says "He took Peter, John, and James and went up on the mountain to pray. As He prayed, the appearance of His face was altered, and His robe became white and glistening. And behold, two men talked with Him, who were Moses and Elijah, who appeared in glory and spoke of His decease which He was about to accomplish at Jerusalem. But Peter and those with him were heavy with sleep; and when they were fully awake, they saw His glory and the two men who stood with Him. Then it happened, as they were parting from Him, that Peter said to Jesus, "Master, it is good for us to be here; and let us make three tabernacles: one for you, one for Moses, and one for Elijah"— not knowing what he said or what he was doing. While he was saying this, a cloud came and overshadowed them; and they were fearful as they entered the cloud. And a voice came out of the cloud, saying, "This is my beloved Son. Hear Him!" When the voice had ceased, Jesus was found alone. But they kept quiet, and told no one in those days any of the things they had seen."

When I opened the door of the bedroom and everyone fell or crawled into the courtyard outside. We looked down the street to where the church was to see if we could see a cloud of God resting on the Church.

God is so very real and He wants to reveal himself to us if we let Him. He is not just a story in a book. He will show himself to anyone who believes. The book of John says, the world cannot see me but you see me because I live inside of you. Because I live, you also will live. On that day you will realize that I am in my Father, and you are in me, and I am in you. The one who loves me will keep my commandments and be loved by my Father, and I too will love them and reveal myself to them that believe."

At this point we were all on the ground outside in the court yard. I managed to crawl over to the gate. Ricky was already there looking down the street through the bars. He said, "LOOK, there is the Cloud of God!" I turned my head to peer down the street to see the church. It was true, there was a cloud that had come down from the sky and rested on the church! Was my vision in the bedroom coming true or was it for a time to come? I had never experienced this kind of thing before, nor have I ever heard of it before other than in the Bible or the movies with special effects added.

We were all so much under the mighty hand of God in the courtyard that none of us really cared about what we looked like, who saw us, or even what time it was. We were out there for hours on the ground getting empty of all the dirt and grime that had rested on the shelves of our lives. A great heavenly fire hose was released, and then God filled us up with His power.

I come up so short in my explanation of all that happened, as I really don't believe there are words to describe what it was like on that day. Have you ever tried to explain color to a blind person? How, when they have never seen before? How can you explain a breathtaking sunset? You just can't tell it. This is my lame attempt at explaining this experience, because it had to be felt from within. He who has eyes to see, look deep, because the kingdom of God is within you.

We struggled to get back in the house to get ready for church, which started at nine in the morning. I don't know if anyone said a word while getting ready. Every time we tried, tears would fill our eyes and the flood gates would release. God's presence was so thick; I was not sure what church would look like if we ever got there.

18 – Confirmation

After such a powerful morning, we finally pulled ourselves together enough to put our clothes on and attempted to walk down the street toward the church. We were ruined for the ordinary; we could just not go on as usual, because we were all shaken to the core by the mighty Wind of God.

Speaking of the Wind of God, I must tell you of an extraordinary event that happened in The United States just before the trip overseas. This is truly an encounter that will not be forgotten, because it is direct confirmation that God was with us.

Anne was seeking God in connection with what He wanted to do through us while we were on the island. This incident happened in her home a week before we left.

She had been praying for some time, when her eyes grew very heavy for she was on the edge of falling asleep. When all of a sudden she arose to what sounded like a helicopter was about to land in her bedroom. She said that the wind force that came with it seemed to consume every square inch of the room that she was in. It was so strong that it lifted the sheet up and down all around her. She so wanted to grab the blanket next to her up around her neck for comfort, but felt paralyzed to do so. It was not a terrifying fear that kept her from moving, but an awesome reverent fear, not from what was happening, but from who was making it happen. Although scared of the presence of this mighty one called "The Wind," she mumbled, "Lord I will go with you wherever you want to take me." Then out of nowhere, she felt a kiss on her right cheek. She wanted desperately to turn and catch a glimpse of His face, but felt frozen by her trembling body. Although short lived, a sweet peace filled the room as it all came to a close.

We always confirm dreams and visions through the Bible. In Ezekiel 3:12 it says, "The Spirit lifted me up, and I heard behind me a loud rumbling sound as the glory of the LORD rose from the place where it was standing. It was the sound of the wings of the living creatures brushing against each other and the sound of the wheels beside them, a loud rumbling sound. The Spirit then lifted me up and took me away, and I went in bitterness and in the anger of my spirit, with the strong hand of the LORD on me." What a powerful confirmation Anne was given by the Holy Spirit.

When we got to the church, we all felt as if we were floating on air. Someone spoke to me but I heard though muffled ears, almost like I was drunk. Out of respect I nodded when I looked at my friends that were with me, they were gone, at least out of this realm anyways.

Before the sermon we had a song service of worship, but it only sailed us higher and higher into the air like a beautiful balloon! By the time worship was over we were ruined completely! I barely heard Ricky say, "Before you are seated please find someone you don't know and welcome them" With such a, powerful move of God upon us, we could barely breathe let along find our neighbor and hug their neck. I had to speak to myself, "Come on Renee, compose yourself." You have a sermon to preach, for heaven's sake!"

19 - On Stage

I slowly stepped on stage and took the microphone, but I had no idea of what I was even going to say. We had just tasted filet mignon with lobster that morning, and it was going to be very hard to go back to a spam sandwich. In other words, when Jesus Christ himself steps out of heaven and meets you in your bedroom, and brings with Him, wind, visions, and empowerment. Well, it's just hard to go back to your average same old; nothing changes, church service, that's all.

I looked out at the herd of sheep in front of me and I began to tear up. I said, "We've had an incredible morning, God has visited us." I shared briefly about how much He loves us, and how he desires for us to know Him. With that said, it was over: I did not use my original sermon notes, and the Holy Spirit was so tangible that people started crying in their seats. You could reach out and touch Jesus, for He was there, in the aisle! My Power Sisters checked out when they first arrived, and all went sailing away to a secret place, so they were of no help to me. I then asked the crowd, "Who wants to be ruined for the ordinary?" That's when Gods power came down! All of the sheep fell on the floor pouring out their desires to Him. I cannot in words even begin to explain what happened on that morning. Christ came down in the church to a very hungry people, and that's where we ate with Him at His banquet table. Once again we came hungry like the children and He fed us from His table Revelation 3 "Behold, I stand at the door and knock; if anyone hears and listens to my voice and opens the door, I will come in to him and will eat with him, and he will eat with me."

When God's power came down that day it was not because of any great preaching skill. It was because He loves people and wants them to rest on Him and what He can do, not on man's ability. In 1 Corinthians 2:1 it says this very thing. "When I came to you, I did not come with eloquence or human wisdom as I proclaimed to you the testimony about God. I came to you in weakness with great fear and trembling. My message and my preaching were not with wise and persuasive words, but with a demonstration of the Spirit's power, so that your faith might not rest on human wisdom, but on God's power." He took the words right out of my mouth!

This was the greatest move of God that I have witnessed and participated to date, but I know the best is still to come, and I can't wait!

20 ~ Twisted Creatures

As everyone was crying out for more of God, a woman named Karen came up wailing and fell to the floor in front of me. She was able to mumble out the words, "I have sinned." I knew she had a very controlling spirit that dominated over both women and men. Many people were afraid of her; for she reminded me of the mafia father that ruled with an iron fist. He plays in the movie called "The God Father." Let me tell you what we believe made Karen grow to be so powerful.

Karen had no place to live, so the pastor cleaned out the back of church, and set up a little apartment for her. Then he gave her all the keys to the church doors and gates. This is a prophetic picture of what happened in the spirit realm: The enemy wanted the spiritual keys to everyone's heart. He would use Karen to be his pawn, to lock them all up. This great entrustment is where the super stronghold of pride, arrogance, and manipulation came into her. For the power of holding the keys went to her head. The enemy set up his campsite right here to begin his battle strategy. He started building in her thoughts; "Karen, you have all the keys, no one else is trusted like you are." He was laying down his foundation to build on; first power, then he moved to possessiveness, manipulation, bitterness, malicious talk, anger and ultimately she, or they, took over.

I will give you a little background of her life. One night around five o'clock a youth went into her room there at the church and saw a huge black spirit lying across her bed. The youth was so terrified that the whole street woke up and got no sleep that night. It took weeks to calm down the teenager so she would not be afraid. Another churchgoer had a dream of her turning into the devil. One man walked into the church to pray and saw green, slimy, twisted creatures with arms and legs going in all different directions up in the rafters of the church, staring at him as he entered. Regardless of the warning signs, these evil spirits got stronger and stronger until the whole community was scared of her (or the demons that were in her).

God warned us in Genesis to master our feelings before they rule us; we have the power to take them hostage. We must not think very long on bad feelings or they will fester on us like boils. "The Lord said to Cain, "Why are you angry? And why do you look sad and depressed and dejected? If you do what is right, will you not be accepted? And if you do not do what is right, sin crouches at your door; it desires to have you, but you must master it." And Cain said to his brother; "Let us go out to the field". And when they were in the field, Cain rose up against Abel his brother and killed him.

He tells us to cast down arguments and every high thing that exalts itself against the knowledge of God, bringing every thought into captivity to the obedience of Christ, and being ready to punish all disobedience. 1 Corinthians 10:5 (ASV)

Karen did what Cain did; she allowed her thoughts to overcome her and so ruled with an iron fist as she claimed rights to the church, the people and the pastors like a goddess. Because of this tremendous role that she played, she tied up the church like a ball of yarn, and tossed it out like a cat and mouse game. It became very satanic. I looked at Jean and she looked at me; we knew it was going to be a fight till the bitter end with these spirits.

Karen was on the floor screaming as if she was in excruciating pain, for the devil came up into her face and twisted it like a rubber band. We put on our boxing gloves as this blasted thing had been there so long that its talons had sunk deep into the walls of the church. You might be asking how the devil comes into a person who is a believer and a church goer. Well, it's like this, the devil transforms into many different entities to deceive us and gain access. Karen started out by giving her life to Christ, and then she started going to church; remember the keys she was given to all the doors? Then she started to complain about the leaders with a group of others. What they thought were merely small meaningless conversations, were gathering more and more fuel for the big fire that was starting to crackle and breathe smoke. They were not at all aware of the devil setting a trap for them; he had been peering in the grass behind their round table discussions like a hungry lion. He was crawling ever so slowly up to them, to purr into their ears. As he snuck closer and closer, he was rubbing his sharp piercing claws together, anticipating his next move. Then he snarled, and with saliva running down his contorted face, he looked for the opportunity to pounce on his victim. He saw his opportunity; it was a crack in the foundation of her salvation. The door was swung wide open, and he slithered like a snake with a whole pride of lions into Karen's house, without her even knowing it.

Meanwhile other lions in the neighborhood smelt the aroma of the roast, and came to participate in the feast. Karen had no idea that this was happening to her.

A similar thing happened to King Saul in the scriptures, "The Spirit of the LORD departed from Saul, and a distressing spirit troubled him. And Saul's servants said to him, "Surely, a distressing spirit is here."

The Bible also says in Numbers 21:5 that they spoke foolishly against God and Moses and said, "Why have you brought us up out of Egypt to die in the wilderness? There is no bread! There is no water! And we detest this miserable food!" Then the LORD sent venomous snakes among them; they bit the people and many Israelites died. The people came to Moses and said, "We sinned when we spoke against the LORD and against you. Pray that the LORD will take the snakes away from us." So Moses prayed for the people.

"Keep watch for the devil roams around like a lion roaring in fierce hunger, he is seeking someone to seize upon and devour." 1Peter 5:8

All of a sudden Karen curled up her lip and growled at us. Jean and I were holding her arms down, for she had become very violent. Reba came over to help us, for Karen needed our whole team, but the rest of the power team was praying for others. These demons were so strong; and they were putting up a tremendous fight, for they did not want to lose their home. As Reba and I prayed, I noticed my arms stinging, and so did Reba. When we looked down at our arms we both noticed big long bleeding scratches. We just looked at each other: Karen's arms were held down by us, there was NO WAY she could scratch us, so what had? I felt as if I was on the brink of hell itself, because an unseen animal (a LION?) was mauling us! As we looked at our wounds I thought, "What a nightmare!" It was seriously scary, but we put our armor back on and returned to the battlefield.

The fight lasted about an hour and forty-five minutes, and then finally it ended! They had lost their grip on Karen, by the Power of the Holy Spirit! Angels had won the victory and dragged their beat up fuzzy dead bodies out of her house. She said she felt very exhausted, typical of a major power struggle. We too were weary and bruised, but with sweat on our brow we stood with our swords raised toward heaven, victorious in our God!

21 - Dreams

God will give us dreams to warn, confirm, direct or propel us into the future. We all have them, but most people feel like they don't have any meaning at all. Some think that it is all about bad food that somehow they digested wrong from the night before. Others say that they never dream, but in reality we all do, almost every night. Most of us just never remember what we dream about, so we write it off as never dreaming at all. God has made us very unique by giving us dreams. Our subconscious takes in our daily affairs and while we sleep, things are being worked out; otherwise we would have nervous breakdowns.

Through the years growing up, I had dreams of people and events that would materialize while going about my day. At first, before I knew anything about dreams, I thought I was having Déjà vu. Déjà vu is a French word meaning, "already seen." It is the phenomenon of having the strong sensation that an event, or persons, that we have met currently, has already been experienced; leaving us feeling like somehow this citation or event has happened before. This is how I was feeling after I would wake up, for I would see someone I thought I knew out on the street, but in reality, I had never met them before. What I did not know is that I probably had a dream about them.

I started inquiring from the Bible as to the meanings of my dreams; because I knew that there were several people in the Bible who had them. Any time that someone in the Bible dreamt, it seemed to have a meaning to it. When they inquired of God as to what it meant, He would give them the interpretation. Therefore, I thought this was a great source to turn to.

I once had a dream that I was in a doctor's office, and behind the glass window where they give you a clipboard of papers to fill out, was a woman who was crying. She was wearing a peach short sleeved sweater and a pair of khaki slacks. I noticed that she was leaning her head down on her desk. I walked up to her in the dream and asked her if she was alright. She said, "No, I'm not!" and burst into tears. I immediately started to pray for her, and then I awoke from the dream.

In real life I was having sinus trouble, so I made an appointment with an ENT doctor. I had never been to this place before, so I was unfamiliar with the layout of the building. I saw that it had several floors so I needed to look at the address that I had, and take the appropriate elevator to my floor. As I was standing in the elevator waiting for the door to close, a woman called out, "HOLD THE ELAVATOR!" I quickly thrust my foot in the door to hold it open for her, when in walked the woman I had seen in my dream! I thought, "SHUT UP!" To add more stress to the story, she was wearing the same clothes that she had on in the dream! For Real?

She kindly asked me to press 3 for her floor, but I was frozen in position. I could not believe this woman was not only the one I had dreamt about the night before, but was also wearing, the very same clothes as she had been in the dream! I pressed 3 with a fixed glance on the woman, and the elevator started to move up. I thought God, what do I do? What do I say? Before I could get my thoughts in place, the elevator opened, and she got out. I was in complete shock as to why I had had a dream about this particular woman.

The elevator took me up to the next floor, and I got off to find my ENT office. I searched the whole floor, but my office was not on that floor, so back in the elevator I went. I ended up going down one floor to 3 and got off in a trance-like state, still in complete wonderment as to what had just taken place in the elevator.

Exhausted from my thought life, my eyes fixed on the door that said ENT, relieved, I walked into the office. I tried to just shake it off for the mean time and just get to my appointment. Because this was my first visit, I went to the window to get the new patient forms to fill out. The woman at the desk pulled back the glass window and handed me the clip-board. My heart jumped inside me, for IT WAS HER AGAIN! It was the WOMAN in my dream! NO WAY! What was happening to me, I was coming unglued, I was shaking! With eyes a glaze, I cautiously took the clip board from her and went to sit down. I needed air, for I was having a HOT FLASH!

What was God saying to me? Trembling in my seat, I sat in quiet prayer to God, "Do I tell her Lord? Lord, they will call the police? I did role-plays in my mind over and over again. I said to myself, "Excuse me, you don't know me, but I had a dream about you last night," or, "I know this is weird, I don't normally dream about people I don't know, but I had a dream about you, last night". Ok, I thought it doesn't matter what I say, it all sounds "handcuff worthy" to me! I sighed deeply, because I did not know what I should do with this dream. If I could just focus on this paperwork in front of me I'd be good. I kept saying "Renee, FOCUS, just focus." I needed Ritalin!

Feeling like a jackhammer, my nerves riveted; I ejected from my seat and fell to the closed window. She looked at me and slid back the glass. "May I help you?" she said. I got so scared, I almost threw up. Then I said, "Uhhh, no I was just looking for a magazine." She pointed to the other side of the room that's when I cut my eyes over to a huge rack right where I had been sitting. Puzzled by my abruptness, she shut the window, with raised eyebrows.

I filled out the paperwork in record time, and marked "no" on every box, whether it applied or not. Who knows what I said was wrong with me. Anticipation was killing me, for I could not concentrate, knowing the woman behind that glass had been in my dream! Again I got up and headed to the window, this time delirious from seriously high blood pressure!

She was just looking at me as I approached the window once again. She said, "Are you done with your paperwork?" "Yes, here it is" I said, and I handed her the papers. She said, "Thank you," and started to close the window, but I suddenly heard the "Halleluiah

Chorus" sounding!! I grabbed the window and held it open, and before I knew what was happening, my heartbeat went into my mouth and I blurted out, "I have to tell you this! I had a dream about you last night!" There, I said it!

With that, she said, "Excuse me just a minute," and went to the back of the office behind a corner so I could not see her! I don't know what she did back there, but she was gone for an awfully long time. My imagination was going crazy! All I kept thinking was that she was probably pushing a panic button that says "Weirdo Alert"! I was expecting for them to come out with a strait-jacket, or men in blue suits to appear with a cot! Surely if someone said this to you, would you not have had all of your fingers at once on 911? Sure you would!

Well, after what seemed like an eternity had passed, she came back out to the front of the office and said, "Sorry about that, now, what was it you said? "I said it again: I know this is extremely strange, but I had a dream last night, and YOU were in it. You were sitting right there, in that chair that you are in now; dressed in the exact clothes that you have on! In the dream, you had your head on your desk and you were crying. I have to ask you "Are you ok?" She looked completely shocked and paused for a long time before saying, "Well, last night I had a lot of pressure on me, and feeling completely overwhelmed from my family situations and work, I laid my head on my desk and cried." I continued, "God wants you to know he saw you crying last night, and cares for you deeply. Also in the dream I prayed for you. Would that be ok, if I prayed for you right now?" I was not at all worried about her response, for I felt God rising up in me. Apprehensive she said, "Now? Ah, okay I guess that will be alright, just let me come out there." As she was on her way out into the patient waiting area, the nurse from the back came through the door and said, "Miss Fotch, the doctor will see you now." Relieved, the woman in my dream said, "Oh, it's time for the doctor to see you!" I said, dejected, "okay, I will keep you in my prayers." She nodded, and I was whisked off to a patient room.

Since then, my dreams have increased dramatically. "In the last days, Again God says in Acts 2:17, I will pour out my Spirit on all people. Your sons and daughters will prophesy, your young men will see visions, your old men will dream dreams." I am not sure whether I am young or old, for I have seen visions, but also have had many dreams. God has promised us in His Word, that if we seek, we shall find. Knowing this, right after I have a dream, I go to Him in prayer, and ask Him for the interpretation. He is faithful to download information about people, places, and things to me. He brings my memory back to past, present, and future things going on in life. Most of our dreams are eighty percent about us, and life all around us, including our friends and family. The other twenty percent could possibly be about future events, and or Bible prophecy being revealed. This is why it is important to not discredit your dreams, for God could be unraveling mysteries to your spirit about yours or someone else's life. However we dream, everything is filtered through the Bible's wisdom, and the powerful Holy Spirit who knows ALL things, which makes His interpretation extremely accurate.

Both Anne and I together share dreams and prophecies that God has revealed to us throughout our everyday lives. It is such a treasure to have a sister and friend who listens to the Holy Spirit as He downloads to her spirit. Jean has also has had incredible dreams that have profound meanings. I will share one with you in chapter 23. God used this particular dream to stop the devil's assignment. It is Incredible!

22 - God Speaks

Every day God speaks to us but men are too busy to perceive what He has said. He uses everything on earth to get our attention, but it takes faith to grab the conversation. He uses children, animals, people and circumstances to speak powerful truths to us. We must train ourselves to look deeper into our everyday affairs, for He is talking to us continuously. He gently pulls back the veil from our natural eyes so that we can see though our spirits to what is really being said. When He was on earth, He only spoke to people using parables or stories. This is so that those that heard had to train their minds to think spiritually instead of naturally. It takes practice to do this, for even His disciples struggled to see deeper than the story at hand, until Jesus taught them how to. We are prone to see with our natural eyes and draw a conclusion. I once saw a clip from a movie that will I never forget. I will share it with you.

There are two men Stan and Chris. Chris is a Christian and lives by faith, while Stan does not believe that God exists. They are standing next to a table when Stan very defiantly tries to defend his position by telling Chris that God does NOT exist! Chris however tells Stan that God uses people to do His will, and that it takes FAITH to believe that He IS.

Stan, mad as fire, puts his paper cup on the table in front of him and starts yelling at Chris, "If God is so real, tell him to make this cup fall off table! He can't do it, can He?" Then looking up at the ceiling, he yells, "Come on God! Just move the cup! Make the cup fall, and then I'll believe! He can't do it, can he Chris? No, He can't! That's because he doesn't exist! Come on God, you do miracles right? Then make the cup FALL!" Then he looks back at Chris and yells, "Some God you serve, He can't even make a simple cup come off the table! That's because he does not exist!"

Chris just looks at Stan and says, "That's because it takes faith to believe in Him. He does not have to prove himself to us. It takes faith to believe. He also uses people to help us believe, and to do His will." Stan pounds his fist in the air and storms out of the room, but on his way out, he trips over the table leg in front of him before exiting. The table wobbles, and the cup falls to the floor"!

Go deeper!

23 - Interpretations

"God speaks again and again, though people do not recognizes or perceive it. He speaks in dreams, in visions of the night, when deep sleep falls on people as they lie in their beds. He whispers in their ears and terrifies them with warnings." Job 33:14-18

We were very tired from the heat, so we all lay down and took a short siesta before continuing our day. We had been invited to go later on that night to someone's house to eat and fellowship, so this rest was a gift.

The room was dark and cool, the perfect place for a nap. It was here that God was revealing mysteries to Jean as she slept. We awoke, and had just started moving around when Jean said, "I just had a very strange dream, and I just can't shake it." Anne and I love this kind of thing because we know that God speaks through dreams quite frequently. Especially because this island was full of spiritual happenings, we wanted to definitely pay attention to any signs that He might have been giving us.

Jean's dream was as follows:

Ricky, Reba, their children, the five of us, and Jenny and her husband from next door, were all at the bottom of a hill. We were all going up to the top of the hill to eat. On our way up, Jenny was called away, down a separate pathway, by a man that no one recognized. She had left the group of us to go with this man. This man wanted her to run away with him and leave her husband, but she said no and came back to the group of us. The man left for a minute, but then returned with a gun to kill Jenny and her husband. He grabbed her arm, swung her around, and pointed the gun at her, then said, "Come with me!", but she would not go. Then out of nowhere he pulled the trigger, and killed her! When the gun went off, Jean leapt up from her bed and awoke! It left her feeling eerie from all the blood pooling around Jenny!

As we were discussing whether the dream had any meaning at all, Reba walked into the room and said, "What are you guys talking about?" When we told her about the dream, she was blown away, because she had been counseling with Jenny about this very issue. Right then, Reba ran out of the room as if she had an emergency bathroom trip. Within a few minutes she returned to our room with Jenny. When they entered the room, we were still all sitting on the floor talking about the meaning of the dream. Reba said, "Jean, can you tell Jenny the dream you had?" Jean said, "Sure," and shared the dream with her.

When Jenny heard the dream, the interpretation became very clear to her as well. She fell on her knees and started crying. That's when she unloaded all that she had been doing prior to this dream. Before we had arrived on the island, she had confided in Reba about a past boyfriend who had been contacting her via Facebook. The relationship was getting more and more serious, for this guy wanted to see her really bad. He was getting very jealous of any kind of relationships that she had with other people. He had made an appointment to meet with her, the very afternoon that Jean had the dream about her. There was just one problem, she was married and her husband knew nothing about any of it.

After she heard the dream, she knew she had to end the entire relationship with this guy. She repented for keeping anything from her husband and asked God to forgive her for the internet affair.

The dream interpretation revealed that God knew all that was happening and wanted to get her attention, and so He gave her life details to a stranger. The dream revealed that death would come to her marriage if she would have met that man that night. God had warned her?

Genesis 41 speaks about how we in ourselves have no power to interpret dreams, but when we inquire of God for his help, everything becomes very clear: A King had a puzzling dream in the Bible and searched for someone to interpret it. The King found out that Joseph had power to interpret dreams, but Joseph revealed to him that he could not. He told the King that God alone holds the meaning behind a dream, but when we ask Him, He will reveal it to us.

Also in the book of Daniel 2:21 it says as a confirmation, "He gives wisdom to the wise and knowledge to the discerning. He reveals deep and hidden things; He knows what lies in darkness, and light dwells with Him. The God in heaven reveals mysteries. He has given us wisdom and power, He has made known to us what we have asked, and He has made known to us the meaning of the dream."

24 - Nightmares

Some dreams or nightmares we want to forget on purpose. I remember one that left my whole body trembling, and I needed prayer to shake it off me. When you have those kinds of dreams you need to get prayer, for they can plague your mind for hours during the day.

"A word was secretly brought to me; my ears caught a whisper of it. Amid disquieting dreams in the night, when deep sleep falls on people, fear and trembling seized me and made all my bones shake. A spirit glided past my face, and the hair on my body stood on end. It stopped, but I could not tell what it was. A form stood before my eyes, and I heard a hushed voice." Job 4:15

There are several things that can trigger unwelcome visitors in our dream life, leaving us terrified to even go to sleep. I remember the day that I went with some friends to get away for the weekend. We had all checked into a nice hotel, and then went to dinner. When we came back to the hotel, we were all exhausted so we went to bed. During the middle of the night I woke to chocking and gagging. Something or someone had my throat. I could not breathe; I was so frantic, that it woke up everyone in the room to start praying immediately! After it left me, I stood in awe of the power that my friend's prayer brought to me. I had forgotten to pray over the room when we first arrived, but vowed never to do that again! We had no idea of whom or what had been there before we had. We have no idea of the spirits that people might have had attached to them that had been in the room prior to us.

There is a good healthy fear that we all have; it's the fear of dying. This is helpful, so that we will not run out in front of a car and die. There is also a healthy, yet terrifying fear that we get when God reveals catastrophic events in a dream. Abram had one of these terrifying dreams, in Genesis 15: 12-13 "As the sun was setting, Abram fell into a deep sleep, and *a thick and dreadful darkness came over him.* Then the Lord said to him, "Know for certain that for four hundred years your descendants will be strangers in a country not, their own and that they will be enslaved and mistreated there."

I went to bed early one night because I was not feeling well. I had chest pain, but it didn't seem like anything major: sometimes if I have too much caffeine it brings unwanted heart palpitations to me. I felt the pain increasing the longer I lay there. I was just a little worried, but managed to fall asleep. I was dreaming that I was sinking into a pit and a black hole was swallowing me. About thirty minutes later I woke up thinking that I was having a heart attack, and I started to hyperventilate. I had a shortness of breath and sat straight up in bed. I thought I was dying, and started to shake and tremble. Before I knew what was taking place, I had my friend call 911. That's when the paramedics showed up and hooked me to a heart monitor. The heart monitor was to confirm that I was not having a heart attack, but rather a panic attack. I had never had a panic attack before and I certainly never wanted another one, for sure! The enemy caused a deep dreadful darkness to come over me, called fear; I was a complete nervous wreck.

The next couple of days I was terrified of everything around me. Fear had entered me when I first felt the chest pain before I went to sleep. It then jumped into my dream life, terrifying me to a panic attack! This is what it looked like: I went to work that next day, but I was scared to death to ride in my car, but then again I was scared not to. I was scared to be in and scared to be out! I was literally in a battle inside myself, from fear of everything! I made a quick dash to the phone to call Jean and see if she would take me to a prayer meeting. I needed to go immediately, for I knew something had happened to me, and it was not natural. She looked up on the internet if any church in the area was having one and we went. I was desperate! When something out of the blue happens like that to me, I know that it is from another realm, and it was not hanging out with me. Oh no, not for even a single minute longer!

The next day, I found myself once again petrified from everything around me. I was desperate to get to a prayer meeting, for I had never felt like this before in my life. I knew that it was from that nightmare, and I knew it was fear. That was very clear to me, but I also knew it was from hell!

Fear had attached itself to me like a snake! I don't know about you, but I hate snakes! I live in a wooded yard filled with leaves, trees and bushes all around my house. I have no doubt that there are a countless number of snakes hiding all curled up under all those leaves. Even though I hate them, I am NOT going out into the yard, to dig through, and hunt them all down, absolutely not! They will stay hidden, but if one dare show himself, that will be his last day on this earth! Fear is very real, it leaves a person feeling paralyzed unable to fight on their own. It is imperative that they have someone fight for them.

I knew that this panic attack was fueled by my thinking about it so I needed to regroup my thoughts. I needed more than one person to pray for me. I needed a team of people to pray. Sometimes we need a group of people to pray to expel the darkness from around us.

Remember the U tube video I spoke about on page 7 of a pride of lions and a group of water buffalo? This is the rest of the story: The baby water buffalo went off by himself to a watering hole. Lions were crouched down in the tall grass by the water, watching the group of animals for an opening. All of a sudden, they made their move to take down the unsuspecting baby buffalo. Every one of the lions together pounced on it and dragged it into the water to kill it. Just then a crocodile lurking in the muddy water grabbed the calf's leg and there was a tug of war for the baby calf. Meanwhile, the team of nearby buffalo heard and saw the problem going on. Just then, every single buffalo went to the rescue of the calf. They gathered around the lions to make a massive wall. Then, probably the mother of the calf fearlessly charged the lions! The lions, amazed by the presence of the pack of buffalo, backed off in fear of them, and left the calf to once again join the group. What a battle! The baby buffalo looked like a goner, from not just the ferocity of the lions but also the crocodile. When the team got together as one, and in complete unity, they became a mighty force to be reckoned with, but by themselves, they were no contest. Hmm, what can we learn here?

Finally, I felt something release me and then I asked God to forgive me, for not having faith but fearing. A panic attack is all about fear! We might fear death, for instance, then we start to breathe heavily, and then panic joins in to make a full-blown panic attack.

We can overcome fear with God's powerful Word. I have included some of the most powerful swords of choice, ones that you can thrust into the air to slaughter the enemy, fear. They are very sharp Swords that you can use if fear comes near you. Pray, and say these scriptures out loud, SWISHHHHHHHHHH.

SWORD 1: "He will cover you with his feathers. He will shelter you with his wings. His faithful promises are your armor and protection. Do not be afraid of the terrors of the night, nor the arrow that flies in the day. Do not dread the disease that stalks in darkness, nor the disaster that strikes at midday. Though a thousand fall at your side, though ten thousand are dying around you, these evils will not touch you." (Ps 91:4-8)

SWORD 2: "Love has no fear, because perfect love expels all fear. If we are afraid, it is for fear of punishment, and this shows that we have not fully experienced his perfect love." (1 Jon 4:18)

SWORD 3: "Do not fear bad news; they confidently trust the Lord to care for them." (Ps 112:7)

SWORD 4: "But Jesus overheard them and said "Don't be afraid. Just have faith." (Mk 5:36)

SWORD 5: "I prayed to the Lord, and he answered me. He freed me from all my fears." (Ps 34:4)

SWORD 6: "Do not be afraid of them; the LORD your God himself will fight for you." (Duet 3:22)

SWORD 7: "The angel of the LORD encamps around those who fear him, and he delivers them." (Ps 34:7)

SWORD 8: "Jesus told him, "Don't be afraid; just believe." (Mk 5:36)

SWORD 9: "Say to those with fearful hearts, "Be strong, and do not fear, for your God is coming to destroy your enemies. He is coming to save you."(Is 35:4)

SWORD 10: "Fear not; you will no longer live in shame. Don't be afraid; there is no more disgrace for you. You will no longer remember the shame of your youth and the sorrows of widowhood." (Is 54:4)

25 - An Idol

Carla had seen what God had done in her sisters Jenny, Lisa and Lila a few days before, and she too wanted to get all the evil out of her and live for Christ. Carla was not able to come that night, because she had to work. She saw such a world of a difference in her sisters that she could not wait to have that same change in her life. In appreciation for what God had done in her sisters and in expectation of what He would do in her, she had invited us to her home for a huge family feast. She invited all of her friends and relatives, for she wanted all of them to be there when she accepted Christ.

We were all having a great time as we rode in the back of a pickup truck to her home. There was a caravan of us all trailing to Carla's house, for she has a very large family. After a very long smooth drive we suddenly came to a complete stop. At first we did not think anything of it, but after several minutes, we started to notice the air was getting stale and very thick in the truck. It was imperative that we move at all times, for constant air flow was a must because of the serious heat index. Alas, we saw the problem up ahead. There was a huge crowd of people congregated together, at least a mile long. To our great surprise they were pulling a massive painted statue of Mary the mother of Jesus down the middle of the street; she was on the back of a flatbed truck. It was so big it looked like a float in a parade. There was music playing from an intercom system that was connected to the sides of the shrine.

I was raised Catholic, so I am very much aware of the great emphasis on Mary. The Catholicism on that island was distinctively different from the denomination I grew up in. These islanders literally worshiped Mary as a god, while Jesus is merely her son. It looked like a parade of people hypnotized were walking very slowly with fixed eyes, each holding a tiny candle in their hand as they walked. This was an extreme demonstration of what they believed might help their dead relatives cross over. There were multitudes of mourners dressed in black who went in front of this huge precession of people, and they too were holding candles for their dead. They also wore hoods over their heads and walked with their backs humped over to show they were mourning. We were told that we would literally be stoned if we tried to speak to them or break up their religious demonstration, for this was truly a sacred ceremony. Mary the mother of Jesus was the center of their focus. She is also said to be the highly exulted intercessor between the living and the dead. You could hear chanting and lamenting's coming from the people as they slowly walked with their heads down in a deep trance. We had never seen anything quite as focused and determined as this religious parade.

It is interesting how each one of us is raised up as children. It all depends on where our mom and dad go to church that will determine where we go to church. It's not just in church that we follow in their footsteps, but every other tradition that's handed down, from generation to generation. Everything is filtered through Gods Word when it comes to religious beliefs. This does not mean that we are necessarily right in some of the ways or ideas that we have inherited.

I've heard a story about a woman, who had watched her mother through the years make a beautiful dinner that consisted of a roast, potatoes and carrots all in the same roaster. She saw her mother cut off six inches of the end of the roast, put it aside in a bag and then add in potatoes and carrots to make the perfect meal. When she started her own family she took on this tradition. When she went to make her roast, despite not knowing why, she also cut off six inches, discarded it, and put the rest in the roaster to cook all day. One day several years later she was at her mother's; they decided to have the same fabulous meal. While in the kitchen helping prepare the food, she noticed her mother put the whole roast in the pot this time, without cutting off six inches. She asked her mother why she always cut off the end of the roast. Her mother said, "Honey, I cut the six inches off because my roaster was too small, and the roast would not fit in it. I then took the remainder of the roast and gave it to the neighbors, for they did not have any income coming in." You see, just because we were raised up in our parent's traditions does not always make it right.

26 - Religion

"I hate, and I despise your religious festivals; your assemblies are a stench to me. Even though you bring me burnt offerings and grain offerings, I will not accept them." Amos 5:21

My parents raised me in the Catholic Church, I remember going into the beautiful church that I attended as a child and looking at the stained glass thinking "Wow, how gorgeous!" I studied each window of masterpiece and watched as an altar boy would go up to the front of the church and light some candles. Some people were knelt down praying silently, while others would curtsy at the end of an aisle, put a dab of holy water on their forehead, and then sit with their heads bowed in a pew. The priest would welcome everyone and then give a spiritual reading. One or two more readings might be read before a brief sermon. The sermon was usually about one of the Holy Saints from long ago, this may last a whole five minutes. We then prayed from a prayer book that was in the pew in front of us, and repeated the Creed that was said by the priest. Then everyone would get up and go to the front for communion, the priest gave us a wafer and some real wine (I think), but we drank it out of a community cup. After we went back to our pews, one final prayer was said and repeated by the people, and then everyone said, "Amen" or the women might say 'Ahh MEN!'

On my way out of the church, we would stop at the confessional box in the back. I was petrified, but I went in to confess my sins to a curtain. I was hoping that someone was on the other end of that curtain, and hadn't stepped out for a smoke break. Sometimes I would peek behind the curtain to make sure he was really there. After I confessed my sins, I once again dabbed my head with holy water and off I went. I always wondered just how holy that water really was, for it was full of germs!

We sometimes went to Saturday Mass, so it would free us up on Sundays. Some Saturday nights we might see a priest in street clothes, at a local bar, having a few drinks. I thought to myself, and this is the guy (or Man of God) who offers up my sins to God? Seriously?

Now looking back at this island, and what was going on spiritually with evil spirits and ghosts, I could understand why they were so scared. Religion and tradition only leaves us with no power over the enemy when we really need it. Religion is going to church without God, or another way of saying it is that it's like trying to put out an inferno, with only a trickle of water. There is just no power!

One day, I was walking alone on the railroad tracks, and I broke out of the formal prayer, I looked up and said, "God if you are real, I want to know you!" I thought, "Oh boy, am I going to be stuck dead by a lightning bolt?" I was not in a church, and no priest was present, so did I really pray a prayer to God? Even more than this, did He hear it?

When I got back home, my dad met me at the door, and he said, "I need to talk with you." Then he took me into his bedroom and said, "You know we have always gone to the Catholic Church, because my parents did, and theirs parents did, and it keeps going for many generations after them. We had never even read the Bible, or had even taken it to Church for that matter; it was just another book on our shelves, collecting dust." Then he continued, "A friend of mine told me to pick it up and to read it, for it is a love letter from God, to us. He said that this book has Power, that's why the enemy tries so hard to keep it out of our hands and from our eyesight. If he can keep us from reading it, we will never know the truth. That is the truth about believing a doctrine that's made by a man, over believing what He really wants, and that is relationship with us."

I was tuned into everything he said, for this was all true: we had never read the Bible before, because the church did not require it, or even tell us that we should. Because we did not take the initiative, we had no idea what it said. I did notice that very few who attended the church never brought a Bible with them. The very place that the Bible should be of utmost value had no need for it, all because their religious ceremonies blinded them.

My dad had a Bible with him, and showed me many scriptures I never knew as a Catholic.

My dad touched the cross on my neck and said, "See this cross you wear, Jesus died on that for you. He is no longer on it, for he rose again." Then he continued by saying that God wanted to talk to me from the inside of my spirit. And that Jesus wanted to come inside of me and live. "Do you want Him to? He asked. "Yes I do!" I replied. That's when he led me through a prayer.

I had asked God to forgive all my sins, just like as if I had never sinned before. I then asked Jesus to come into me, into my life. He then said "Renee you are now a Christian" I could not believe I could pray just by talking to him like this, I thought prayers had to come from a religious book. I was amazed that it was just that easy! I started crying, for something was stirring inside of me. I did not know what I had done to the fullest by praying that prayer, but I would in the days to come.

To my surprise my dad gave me my very own Bible! This was not just any Bible though, because it was written how I spoke. It was the NAS. I loved it, because it was not boring to me like other Bibles that I had seen; that spoke in Romeo and Juliet style. It speaks like I talk, I loved it!

Religion vs. Relationship

To do something religiously is what we all do whenever we develop a habit, that is, so in a sense we are all religious.

The difference between religion and relationship is: Suppose you found someone who lavishes you with gifts, rewards you with secrets of wisdom, brings you home treasures hidden in darkness, takes care of you when you're sick, protects you from enemies that slander your character, delivers you from all worry and fears, surrounds you with affection when you're feeling down, and catches your tears to keep in a bottle? What if their attributes are too wonderful to describe, can you keep it quiet. Would you not surrender your life to them? Would you not shout from the rooftop your relationship everywhere you go? This is relationship with God. He is an inward best friend that speaks to your spirit through His Word.

With a law there is no threat to those that keep it, but it is a threat for the ones who are bent on breaking it. For instance, if a righteous believer sees a cop on the street (God) there is no fear for he knows he has done nothing wrong to receive judgment. But on the other hand if you are doing drugs and see the same cop (God) there is a deep fear that comes over you because you are breaking the law. So you move away from the cop and keep your distance for fear he could sense something is wrong with you or recognize your face, then arrest you.

Religion is this: a set of rules, regulations, dos and don'ts, laws, and rituals, and solitude with reverence in a formal atmosphere. Can you not understand why someone would not want to share their faith? Because to the religious, it is an extremely private matter what is reverenced and sacred and should not be talked about outside the church. John 5:39 says "You study the Scriptures diligently, because you think that in them you have eternal life. These are the very Scriptures that testify about me, yet you refuse to come to me to have life."

People in the average church would be scared stiff if demons were to manifest in a service. So ministers stay far away from preaching on any subject that would provoke them to manifest lest they frighten the people to death and they lose their congregations. Some clergy never encourage their people to read their Bibles, or stay away from evil. Some churches are dead and dry and people go out of a sense of duty or obligation, thinking they are doing a holy thing. It makes them feel good, because they've attended church.

Other shepherds only give their sheep a handful of grass to eat and a tricking of water to swallow. The sheep then leave their pastures, starving and thirsting to their death. Other men are only a hireling; they have a form of godliness, but deny the power of God, which is able to rescue men from the pit that they're in. People are then left fending for themselves spiritually and so live in utter defeat, and bound in chains most of their lives. Even worse than this, they are in serious danger of going to hell.

There are only a few godly leaders out there that we can pattern our lives after, ones that live holy not religious lives. It is pitiful! Again Amos 5:39 says, "I hate all your show and pretense the hypocrisy of your religious festivals and solemn assemblies. Instead, I want to see a mighty flood of justice, and an endless river of righteous living."

I am going to describe what God really requires of us. He is not a robot, or a list of do's and don'ts. He is a very personal God. God loves us even if we don't love him. It says in 1 John 4:10, "Now this is love, not that we loved God, but that He loved us." He also wants to provide for our every need when we pray. It is really not by our own hands and power that we have created wealth, it is because of Him. Deuteronomy 8:18 says, "Who fed you in the wilderness with manna, which your fathers did not know? Don't you say in your heart, 'My power and the might of my hand have gained me this wealth for me?' "For you shall remember the Lord your God, for it is He who gives you power to get wealth, that He may establish His covenant which He swore to your fathers, as it is this day."

God is not in heaven looking down, just waiting for us to fail, nor is He so far away that He pays no attention to our pretty little meaningless lives. No, God is very personal; He goes from being Huge by watching nations wage war against each other, to knowing how many hairs fell out of your head today. Matthew 10:29 says "Are not two sparrows sold for a penny? Yet not one of them will fall to the ground outside your Father's care and even the very hairs of your head are all numbered. So don't be afraid; you are worth more than many sparrows."

27 - EYES Wide Open

"I counsel you to buy from me gold refined in the fire, so you can become rich; and white clothes to wear, so you can cover your shameful nakedness; and salve to put on your eyes, so you can see." Revelation 3:18

We had asked God to use us on this trip mightily, but we really had no idea of what he had planned for us. He opened our eyes so that we could see, and that is just what we did. We saw that this island is filled with extremely spiritual people, for the airways are lit up with spiritual forces, unseen by the natural eye but extremely evident to those who have their spiritual eyes open. There was all kinds of evil everywhere we set our eyes. There are evil spirits having fiestas 24/7 throughout the whole land. Because these evil spirits are so welcomed by the people's lifestyles there, they have become so blatant that they literally appear to the people to terrorize them. These people see ghosts! They also have visions, not from God but from, the occult familiar spirits. They operate in witchcraft, cast spells on each other, they use black magic, have séances, and they go to mediums and Spiritist for medicine and also to predict the future.

They don't even realize they are heaping on themselves all kinds of curses, and sicknesses. They have three to four idols in their homes, just adding to the collection to their other gods. They are trying desperately to seek God, but don't know where to look for Him, so they run to the Catholic Church in hopes that they can get enough religion to save them from the devil.

Let's look into our lives and examine it by God's mighty flashlight, His powerful Word. This island is not the only place that is a total spiritual mess; no, this also represents America, the wealthy nation! Demons hide well here, through intellect and reasoning, but since we had been overseas, our eyes have been seriously opened to the spirits that are hiding in people. Now we see things like we have never seen before! We had prayed before this trip for God use us and I believed He did; by opening our eyes to all that's around us.

"When the servant of the man of God got up and went out early the next morning, an army with horses and chariots had surrounded the city. "Oh no, Elisha what shall we do?" the servant asked. "Don't be afraid," the prophet answered. "Those who are with us are more than those who are with them." And Elisha prayed, "Open his eyes, Lord, so that he may see." Then the Lord opened the servant's eyes, and he looked and saw the hills full of horses and Chariots of Fire all around Elisha." 2King 6:5

28 - The Aroma

We finally made our way into Carla's house. Just outside was that huge demonstration in the street, but inside a very special meal was awaiting us. Now this was no ordinary dinner, no, it was an all-out fiesta! When we arrived; there were people everywhere you looked, and more were still coming. I thought, "Have they come because of the demonstration in the street or to support Carla?"

The smell upon entering the home put you in utopia, for there was food and drinks everywhere with a continuous flow of more, coming from the kitchen. They had made a countless number of dishes, from spicy stuffed fish to caviar. They were so honored to have us come into their home, for they had all witnessed the great transformation in Carla's other three sisters. They all wanted to express their gratitude to the fullest. In reality, it was not us they were honoring: no, we were only the vessels. It was Jesus who was the guest of honor that night, for He was and is the mighty deliverer.

Lisa, one of Carla's sisters had been in a deep depression most of her life and could never find a smile. She was bent on rebellion, and even her family found it hard to communicate with her. After prayer the night that she got delivered, her countenance completely changed, and the rebellious attitude left as well! The family was not only amazed at this great change but looked with intensity in her face to see if this was real, for Lisa was a changed woman! The same had happened to her other two sisters as well. Although they had gone to the church for years for they were Catholics, they had never seen anything like this before, for this was not the kind of religion that they were used to...

Carla wanted us to share with her friends and family a message of salvation before dinner, for she too wanted to give her life to this transforming God. The very cool thing was that Ricky and Reba had tried and tried to share with them the message that God is not a religion, but to no avail. It took a demonstration of power to change them, for when they saw Ricky and Reba walk through their doors they had an unbelievable respect that they had never showed them before.

They gathered from everywhere to meet with us in the living room. They were crammed in the kitchen, the yard, and in back rooms and hall ways; as many as could fit were there. They don't have glass in their windows, so those outside, pressed against open windows and piggybacked each other so that they might be able to hear the message. About thirty had crammed themselves on the tiny porch outside and even carried into the street to get within hearing distance. We were totally blown away at how many people were there for this event. Delicious, scrumptious smells that made your mouth water were penetrating the atmosphere around us and Jean was prepared to share. I thought like most Americans, "Oh no, the food is hot and Jean is up to bat," but amazingly they were not focusing on the piping hot savoring food in front of them, but wanted to hear the message. Here is an interesting scripture: "To one we are an aroma that brings death; to the other, an aroma that brings life." 2 Corinthians 2:16

Jean shared with them how she found Jesus in an abusive home situation. Every ear and eye in the house was focused on what she had to say. Most of those in the home were either Catholic or just did not go to any church at all. We could see across the room that there were spirits lurking behind some of their eyes, it was uncanny. While Jean spoke, the rest of us prayed under our breath, for the atmosphere was lit on fire because the Word of God was being released and mingled with faith. We could literally see who was receiving the message and who was being tormented in their souls just by looking into their eyes. I could see by their faces that swords were coming out of their sheaths, from angels with us and demons coming out of the woodwork of her home. Something was happening in the spirit realm that we could not see, because people from down the street by the hordes started flooding the front porch. They made such a noise outside that we all turned around to see the massive crowd just trying to peek a view.

Jesus says in John 12:32 "If I be lifted up from the earth I will draw all men to Myself."

Jean shared about how much God loved them, and how he just wanted them to know that no matter what they had done, or where they had been in their lives, no sin was too great to forgive. All they had to do was ask God for forgiveness and receive Jesus into their lives.

Being Catholic they already knew that Jesus had died on the cross. They just did not know that it was for them that He died, making it very personal. If they were the only one on the earth Jesus would have shed His blood for just one of them. The message broke through religious traditions and brought it down to God calls you his sons and daughters. Once they heard this, Carla started crying; and several others joined in with tears they were all under arrest by the Holy Spirit. All but six gave their lives to Christ! Angels had to be singing and doing summersaults in heaven because a wayward child had come home. In Luke 15:10 says, "I say to you, there is joy in the presence of the angels of God over one person who repents." I know that demons were running for their lives, because angels had crashed their party and chased away darkness.

Carla told us that she saw black spirits in her home because of sexual sin; she knew that she had opened a door to let them in. Ricky prayed with her and told her that if she saw any more evil spirits, she was to call us, and we would come back with our swords flaming in the air to get rid them.

The ride back to our house was peaceful, for we were full of delicious food, but worn out from the invisible battle of light and darkness.

29 - Snatched from Hells fire

After intense prayer, we got ready to move on out, for we had a big day in front of us. First we had a Bible study scheduled, and then several children's feedings. Reba and Ricky, the pastors had just been called to another mediums house, this time for healing. It was interesting that all the mediums attended the Spiritist church, but whenever one of them was at death's door they would call Ricky and Reba to see if their God could do anything. They first would try all of their spells, prophecies and witch potions before reverting to calling "The Born-again Church." However this was different: Rita had given her life to Christ, and had made the call for her mother, the medium.

Reba and Ricky had been praying for this family for a long time, they were very happy that we could all accompany them. When we reached the location of the home, we got off the truck and started walking through a twisted back alleyway. It was very wet from leaky plumbing problems, and had a bad smell of spoiled garbage. On our way there, we passed by a black, old weathered tin shed that was completely darkened with a filthy black tarp hanging over it. We were told this was the witch doctors quarters. It was very eerie to pass by this place, as we could see eyes peering out of a small crack in the wall. They followed us as we went next door to Rita's mother's house.

As we entered we saw a woman on a bed of bamboo, with no sheets, and no covers, just raw bamboo wired together to make a bed. Ricky had asked her what was wrong. She went on to explain that for the past four months she had been lying on that cot. She blacked out, in her kitchen while making a cake, and when she finally came to, she could not move her legs. Then the paralysis moved up and affected her head as well; she felt like a prisoner in her own body. She was in need of a complete healing and wanted us to all pray.

Each one of us spoke to her through an interpreter about God and how much he loved her. She started to cry on her bamboo bed, and then yelled to a family member to fetch a rag, to dry her tears. Then she looked Ricky in his eyes, pointed at him and said in her language, "I want to give my life to your God." Ricky turned around and said to us, "She wants to ask Jesus into her life." We were in complete shock; all we had done was walk into the house and say very little! Ricky led her in a prayer to ask God to forgive her of her sins and come into her life. After the prayer, she lay there and just smiled, for she could not move her body. She was clenching her jaw when she spoke, "I am also in a lot of pain." That's when Reba spoke up and said, "God is not done here, now we will pray for healing." By this time the whole community had gathered around this house once again, they were in all the windows and doorways. They all wanted to see if God would raise this woman up.

We prayed and prayed, and head many of them praying as well. Finally Ricky said, "How are you doing?" She began to raise up her head, for the pain had left. "No more pain!" she said. She could not believe it, for pain had been there every hour for the last four months. She could not sleep or cook or get up; all she did was cry. But when God touched her, all the pain left, and her head lifted off the cot, then she sat up! Her family and all those outside were doing flips in the yard, for people were in absolute awe, and amazed in every way! In prayer, we had taken authority over the enemy, and had commanded angels to slice through every sickness and disease with their Swords. That is when it broke! We believe the enemy's chains were not only broken but shattered off of her! We kept praying, for this was just the beginning. Little by little she stood on her feet. Then all by herself she walked across the floor to a chair to rest, for she had not walked in a long time. She was crying for joy, and then she proclaimed, "I'm coming to your church!"

This was absolutely amazing in every way, for the whole clan wanted to come to the church to see this great God! The news of this healing spread so fast that by the time we got to church she had already contacted her five sons and told them, and they too gave their lives to Christ! The church grew in number on that day. Of course there was a time of great celebration, for our God crushed the enemy, and set those in prison FREE!

Because Rita's mother had just received a remarkably huge healing and the whole community was turned inside out, talk of it was everywhere and everyone was starting to believe in Jesus. The people wanted to immediately start a Bible study there because they were all very hungry for some answers. At this Bible study was a woman named Sheena. Sheena had just recently given her life to Jesus as well, however her husband was a warlock and her mother-in-law was a powerful witch; which made life very interesting, to say the least. The witch lived right next door to the house where the Bible study was being held, so there was defiantly a power struggle. Hmmm... Sheena's mother- in-law did not approve of this marriage, and she had made a distinctive distaste to everyone around her, that she was not in favor of it. Sheena was trying desperately to have a baby, but every time she fell pregnant, the baby would be still born. She had a great fear that her mother-in-law was putting a curse on her because of her belief in God. Whenever her mother-in-law saw her, she would tell Sheena that her baby was going to die, in hopes of cursing her seed.

This is the power of our words: the Bible says there is LIFE and death in the power of the tongue. We can curse or bring healing to another just by our words. Even more, when we start to believe what others say about us, it either brings us down or lifts us up. That's why it is very important to always say positive things, and fill our minds with God's life giving words, for negativity and curses will only bring forth death.

The devil hated that she was no longer his and was furious that even more women were getting saved. He knew that he was losing his grip, so he decided to steal their seed by killing the children before they were born. When the mid wife came to try and deliver a third child she froze in fear. She saw a woman in a black hooded garment with a white face standing next to Sheena and snatch the baby from here womb to put it into a coffin next to her, then she disappeared. This was so very creepy that even when we were told of it; it gave us goose bumps. It definitely would make you lose any kind of hope you had if you believed this and took it to heart.

She tried to get advice from her neighbors but they were drowning in their own problems. They gambled everything away in their own homes and all night long they did drugs, drank, smoked, and did lewd sex acts never giving thought to the outcome. The Israelites did something very similar. "When the people saw that Moses was so long in coming down from the mountain, they gathered around Aaron and said, "Come and make us gods who will go before us." As for this fellow Moses who brought us up out of Egypt, we don't know what has happened to him." Aaron answered them, "Take off the gold earrings that your wives, your sons and your daughters are wearing, and bring them to me." He took what they handed him and made it into an idol cast in the shape of a calf, fashioning it with a tool. Then they said, "These are your gods, Israel, who brought you up out of Egypt." Afterward they sat down to eat and drink and got up to indulge in revelry." Exodus 32:1-6

All of these people are under a serious influence of darkness, with demons swarming like flies all around them. Their dark influence and advice would only put more curses on her, so she had no one to turn to but Jesus. When Sheen was religious she was no threat to the Spiritist church, it was when she accepted Jesus Christ that the trouble started. She could mention the word "God" all day long, but once she started saying Jesus, the devils came out in swarms against her.

Now here is where the rubber hits the road: you and I can say God all day long, but it's when we say Jesus that we have a war on our hands. The devil is not threatened by the title "god" for he himself feels like he *is god.* No, it's when you say the name

"Jesus" that's when his kingdom is threatened. He HATES the Name of JESUS, because that's where the POWER is!

People, well not really people, but spirits, are so afraid of this name that they try very hard to snuff it out of everything they can. They do this by taking His name out of schools, courthouses, off of our money, and they also want to remove nativity scenes. As a matter of fact they are attempting to banish Christmas altogether. The word Christ, assaults them terribly, demons hate it, because they know His Name means "Anointed One." Philippians 2:9-11 says, "God exalted Him to the highest place and gave Him the name that is above every name, that at the name of Jesus every knee should bow, in heaven and on earth and under the earth."

Can you see the huge clash of light and darkness in Sheena's house, for Jesus and the devil don't go together. When we got to the Bible study Sheena wanted prayer immediately, because she was now eight months pregnant. We prayed to break every single word curse that had been placed over her life, and also the life of her unborn child, for she was scared to death. Half of the battle was to convince Sheena that these words had no power over her any more. Then we broke generational curses and spells that might be carried down her blood line.

I opened my eyes and looked up, only to see two darting eyes from the broken window next door. Peering through slits in the wood was the witch, staring down at us as we prayed.

Can you see the clashing of two Swords?

30 - The Witch

The witch who was in the small hut next door was glaring at us, in hopes of intimidating us to the tune of "GET OUT OF MY DOMAIN!"

We ended up leaving, but not because of her; when we passed by her tin home she quickly pulled the blinds and shut out the remaining light around her. She did not seem to have any power at all, for all the power that witches or warlocks have is given to them by us, through our fears. They get more and more powerful if they can keep us locked up in fear, but turn on the light and watch them run!

As we moseyed down the street we decided to go house visiting. Some of the residents have built houses from a pile of cardboard. This was home to them, and when we would walk by they welcomed us into their place and treated us like Royalty. One thing we know about them is that materialism is not one of their gods! The prosperity message is a hard sermon to preach here, for it is not easily swallowed when you have nothing. As discouraging as it might seem, for poverty is staring at you from all directions, there is still hope; His name is Christ.

The Israelites ate manna, it was sent down from heaven every morning, and they also lived in tents for forty years. Daniel was put in the center of a courtyard during a battle, and given a ration of bread every day at the changing of the guards. Elijah was fed by ravens during a famine, so no matter where we are in life, or where we live, if we trust in God and pray, He will provide what we need.

We ended up at another witch's home. Her name is CoCo. We had touched on this lady briefly in part nine, remember the mummies? She was one of the zombie-like people who came to Cary's rescue when we attempted to cast out the STRONGMAN spirit from him. Actually, until that day we had no earthly idea how big this satanic fortress's on this Island was, for it was way out of our league. We knew this had to be God directing us, for we would NEVER have entered this hornets' nest on our own, and that is for sure!

This precious lady had been in the Spiritist church all of her life, and she did not know anything else. When you have been in an occultist church all of your life, all you believe is that you have the truth. You believe that everybody else is wrong, when all the while you may very possibly be the one in error. If what you believe does not go along with the Bible, then it is a lie, for God's Word is TRUTH. The Bible says "Do not believe every spirit, but test the spirits to see whether they are from God, because many false prophets have gone out into the world. This is how you can recognize the Spirit of God: Every spirit that acknowledges that Jesus Christ has come in the flesh is from God, but every spirit that does not acknowledge Jesus is not from God. This is the spirit of the antichrist, which you have heard is coming and is now in the world." 1 John 4

God caused many Christians through the years to come in contact with CoCo to shine a light to her, but the devils inside of her would not allow her to receive their words of life. Her relatives who believed in God, spent many countless hours in prayer for her, over many years, so all of this labor was not in vain. The ground had been cleared dredged by one missionary for three years, and now God had brought in a brand new pastor to plant the seed.

When we went into her house she spoke highly of the last missionary that had been there and the work that he had done while on the island. She respected him highly because of his integrity toward the other islanders. He had witnessed to her every chance that he got about the power and Love of God, but her roots were so deep rooted in the occult that more digging and dredging was required. We heard her story, which ran through generations after generations of blood lines of mediums among her ancestors. She was defiant and very confident in her belief system and not afraid to debate the Bible.

In The Spiritist church they would pray for the sick, and healing would come, not by God, but by the enemy, for the enemy will heal someone so they will put their trust in that church. This is kind of like an animal trap: the bait is there for the inquisitive wanderer, and he joyfully eats, not knowing it is a DEATH trap. The person that may receive a healing would leave the church clicking their heels in the air. Later they may find out that they now have an evil spirit or they could get something worse than they came in with. It was called an exchange.

As I sat in her home, I could literally feel a presence brush by my arm. I looked around and saw people everywhere, they were peering at us through doors and every window to see what was happening to the medium. CoCo never had company for her house was always closed up and dark. We all started to pray for Gods angels to come and assist us, for this was a very spiritual battle.

Anne shared a very powerful testimony, about how the power of God had brought her out of a similar Spiritist church many years ago. She shared about being deceived by lies that kept her in a deep darkness. She told of her days as a tarot card reader and how she felt empowered when she would read others fate. She also spoke about outer body experiences that terrorized her at night. Although fearful, she was intrigued by the power of the dark side. Little did she know that thick spider webs had formed around her soul? She came to the place of wanting to end it all. She left her fate to a phone book: gun in hand, she closed her eyes and opened the phone book for hope, and it landed on a page of churches! Almost illuminating off the page was a Bible believing church with a huge address and phone number! The spirit of God spoke to her spirit, even being in darkness she felt something pulling her, and then it propelled her to go to the church listed in the phone book. Long story short Anne gave her life to Jesus Christ, who saved her from hell. I mean literally! The enemy wanted her to end it all, but God threw her a rope and saved her.

As Anne shed the light about the deep darkness behind mediums, tarot cards, séances, tea leaves, astrology, palm reading, spells, divination, crystals and out of body experiences, you could see the torment coming up in CoCo's face. She started to squirm in her chair, and you could see her eyes changing, for her eyes became fixed on Anne like a cat caught in an alley late at night. She hung on every word that Anne had to say, for she was under the unction of the Holy Spirit's mandate. Anne shared stories with CoCo about all she had done in the darkness. When she started reading tarot cards she felt empowered, for the enemy convinced her that she was unstoppable. This intrigued CoCo for she too was seeking for power beyond this realm. Then Anne shared that darkness grabbed her in the middle of the night. It entered into her dream life and she had an out of body experience that terrified her. The spirit guides that she felt were friendly, all at once turned against her. They clawed at her spirit and terrified her with incredible fear. The house where she had been staying was haunted and things would fly across the room. Anne said, "These are demon spirits of darkness, they are not friendly, CoCo. They want to possess you and then kill you." This woman could see that Anne was the real thing and that her God really had saved her from taking her own life. CoCo looked up in amazement at the pastor next to her, for Anne was speaking her language, although she was using an interpreter. The message went far deeper than a cultural interpretation. The Holy Spirit had her phone number and started revealing the stronghold of deception to her.

The enemy was losing his slimy grip, for CoCo sat straight up and pointed upwards saying, "Yes, I want Cristo!" We all read her body language, and clearly understood the word "Cristo." I said out loud, SHUT- UP! The pastor looked as if someone had slapped him in the face. We were all stunned! We just looked at each other in utter Amazement! I thought "Seriously, after all these years?"

Darkness was stumbling trying to get out the door so fast that it was tripping us on its way out. This was so incredible to see, for a brilliant ray of light literally shot through the house like a sword. It was like a cloud was pulled back from the sun at that exact moment. A brilliant ray of light came shooting through the window of the room we were in. I was just standing there in awe of this incredible transformation when I lost my footing. My foot went out from underneath me and I almost fell down, for no reason at all. It was as if I was pushed out of the way, as Angels were thrusting their Swords into fleeing demonic spirits. It must have been so violent when the spirit realm, brushed up against the natural realm, that we felt it.

Charles, the past missionary, was going to flip for joy at this wonderful news! She was a major influential person in the Spiritist church! Ouch, for the kingdom of darkness had just lost an extremely valuable player for his side. Her countenance changed immediately to the biggest smile you can ever imagine! CoCo's daughter was standing right next to her, and she was to crying for joy, as she had prayed for her mother for YEARS! The whole community was affected by this re-birth. This was HUGE!

31 - Choose

Ricky had asked Anne if she would share at the next service, so she prepared a message and we headed out the door to the church. As she got up to share, she noticed Cary, or should I say the demonic strongman that was in Cary, just glaring at her as she spoke. The Holy Spirit became so strong in the service that Cary could not take it, so he abruptly got up and left. The power of God fell on the rest of the people who had come and everyone came forward, crying out for The Holy Spirit to touch them. All of a sudden out of nowhere, Cary came running from the back of the church, and fell on the floor with a clash. We all turned around to look at what had just come through the doors, when Cary started to manifest demon after demon. We immediately started to pray for him, but Cary was doubled over, by angels I'm sure, driving their swords into the evil spirits in Cary. Also the power of God was so very strong in the building that demons had no choice but to submit.

We have often been asked why signs and wonders always happen in other countries. All I know is that here in the US we stand in pride and wealth, and so we feel we have no need of God. He is explained away by our intellect and most believe that we have need of nothing. God says in His word in Deuteronomy 8:17 "You may say to yourself, "My power and the strength of my hands have produced this wealth for me." But remember the Lord your God, for it is he who gives you the ability to produce wealth, and so confirms his covenant, which he swore to your ancestors, as it is today."

Whenever we have gone into a third-world nation we have seen very spiritual people. They call on any and every god that they can to help them make money, heal their bodies and ward off evil spirits. God to them is a necessity; it is imperative that they seek a higher power for help. Because of this, some may carve an idol out of wood or metal, then fall prostrate in front of it and pray. This heap on the ground they would then call god. They end up praying to it, asking it to help them through their everyday lives. Demons love this kind of thing, so they jump right into the mix, causing sicknesses, poverty, depression and deep confusion. Although they may be ignorant of the knowledge of the truth, the enemy uses it to build a fortress of witchcraft. The Bible says in Hosea 4:6 "We die from a lack of knowledge." So why should we go and tell them? Romans 10:19 says How, then, can they call on the one they have not believed in? And how can they believe in the one of whom they have not heard? And how can they hear without someone preaching to them? Suppose it were our mom or dad, sister or brother, friend or spouse; would we not want them to believe? Now, who will go?

With this said, when a missionary goes to another country and starts talking about the real God Jesus, that's when things start to happen! The people that live there already have a belief system of sorts set up in them, but their belief is not in the right God, and it is not working. When we bring Jesus to people whether here in the states, or overseas, He just shows up. He doesn't show up empty handed, no, He brings His power with Him! People are not interested in religion; they want something that is REAL. They need a powerful God not a wooden idol that can't do anything for them. Everyone who prays wants to be heard, so let's tell them.

When we take the real God "Jesus" to people, God cannot help but to do great signs and wonders, for He just LOVES people. If we believe in Him then our prayers will pull down serious strongholds, sicknesses will disappear, depression will leave, bondages will break, chains will fall off, addictions will shatter and crumble to the ground, and demons will come out of the woodwork.

I love this story in 1 Kings 18 "Elijah went before the people and said, "How long will you waver between two opinions? If the Lord is God, follow him; but if Baal is God, follow him." But the people said nothing. Then Elijah said to them, get two bulls for us. Let Baal's four hundred and fifty prophets choose one for themselves, and let them cut it into pieces and put it on the wood but not set fire to it. I will prepare the other bull and put it on the wood but not set fire to it. Then you call on the name of your god, and I will call on the name of the Lord. The god who answers by fire—he is God."

Then all the people said, "Ok." Elijah said to the prophets of Baal, "Choose one of the bulls and prepare it first, since there are so many of you. Call on the name of your god, but do not light the fire." So they took the bull given them and prepared it. Then they called on the name of their god Baal, from morning till noon "Baal, answer us!" they shouted. But there was no response; no one answered. And they danced around the altar they had made.

At noon Elijah began to taunt them. "Shout louder!" he said. "Surely he is a god! Perhaps he is deep in thought, or busy, or traveling. Maybe he is sleeping and must be awakened." So they shouted louder and slashed themselves with swords and spears, as was their custom, until their blood flowed.

Midday passed, and they continued their frantic prophesying until the time for the evening sacrifice. But there was no response from their god, no one answered, and no one paid attention.

Elijah took twelve stones, and with the stones he built an altar in the name of the Lord, and he dug a trench around it. He arranged the wood, cut the bull into pieces and laid it on the wood. Then he said to them, "Fill four large jars with water and pour it on the offering and on the wood." "Do it again," he said, and they did it again. "Do it a third time," and they did it the third time. The water ran down around the altar and even filled the trench.

At the time of sacrifice, the prophet Elijah stepped forward and prayed: "Lord, the God of Abraham, Isaac and Israel, let it be known today that you are God in Israel and that I am your servant and have done all these things at your command. Answer me, Lord; answer me, so these people will know that you, Lord, are God, and that you are turning their hearts back again."

Then the fire of the Lord fell and burned up the sacrifice, the wood, the stones and the soil, and also licked up the water in the trench. When all the people saw this, they fell prostrate and cried, "The Lord he is God!"'

32 - Hades

Everywhere we went on this Island we saw evil spirits coming up in people's eyes, for God had opened our spiritual eyes to all the evil around us. There were times when we all went shopping; while we were out we could not make eye contact with anyone at the store. This was because the demons knew who we were and when they saw us from other's eyes, our shopping trip would come to an end. The Bible says "He gave them power and authority to preach the gospel, heal the sick and to drive out all demons." We all like the first two commandments, but who wants to come into contact with evil spirits every day or every hour; for that matter? Yikes! For heaven's sake, I don't know about you, but I HATE scary movies, let alone coming in contact with the real thing!

In these days we can find every scary movie under the sun either playing on TV or at our theaters. There are blood sucking Vampires, murder mysteries, movies about witches, wizards, mediums, exorcists, demon possession and there are hundreds more like this. Notice that they are all mystical and intriguing to draw us to the supernatural, because Satan wants to make it all seem very harmless. None of these movies prepares you for the real thing though! Most people think that it's no big deal, that this is all fake."

I actually was at a flea market shopping when I saw a booth of someone selling wizard wands. They came with instructions on how to successfully cast a spell on your enemies and colleagues just by believing. The enemy uses these things to desensitize us about his evil ways.

One thing I have learned is that the spirit world is more real than this world that we live in. We think if we can't see it, then it must not be there. Hmm, there is a whole world under our feet, right in the heart of the earth. If people could crawl out of the ground and come back from the dead, they would plead with us, "Don't come here!" The devil wants to keep this place a secret; He wants to keep our minds far, far away from that talk. He does not want us to believe that it even exists.

"There was a rich man and a beggar the time came when they both died. The beggar went to heaven but the rich man to Hades, where he was in torment. He looked up and saw Abraham far away, with Lazarus the beggar by his side. So he called to him, 'Abraham, have pity on me and send Lazarus to dip the tip of his finger in water and cool my tongue, because I am in agony in this fire.' "But Abraham replied, 'Son, remember that in your lifetime you received good things, while Lazarus received bad things and you never helped him out? He is now comforted here and you are in agony. "He answered, 'then I beg you, Abraham, send Lazarus back to my family, for I have five brothers. Let him warn them, so that they will not also come to this place of torment." Luke 16:28

I went to New Orleans once; it was one of those mandatory stops while on a cruise ship. This was all before Hurricane Katrina destroyed the city. The street leading up to boarding the ship, was full of palm readers, mediums, psychics, wizards and tarot card readers. Why? Because everyone wants to have their future told to them. Most people think there is nothing wrong with this, so this ended up being one of the busiest streets in that city. People have no idea that this is one of the most dangerous ways to find out about their future. The enemy is like a chameleon, for he changes constantly to deceive his prey; he seeks out those who are just mindlessly wandering around, for they are easy targets.

The enemy may use one of these mediums to share with us one truthful area in our lives, but this is how he ensnares us in an unseen evil trap. He gains our trust, and then he twists and turns the mediums words with fear-based lies.

You see, this deception is greater than a bold faced lie, because we can almost always see through a lie. It is when he tells us the truth first, and then he inserts the lie. Mix it together for the perfect blend of deception. That's when he ensnares us. Now he knows you will believe all his lies! He is very dark; he will tell you something good, but then poison your mind with something bad, like a divorce or a death, or sickness or even a tragedy.

A medium told Anne before she became a Christian that her son would die before he reached his seventeenth birthday. Do you see the seed of fear that he inserted into her? It's a seed of torment; this lie tormented her for years through worry and fear. She was a wreck at every cut or fall or sickness that would come near to him. The enemy intended to kill her son through her believing in his lie of death.

The Bible says that each man has been given a measure of faith. If we feed our faith, it will grow and begin to materialize, so it is very important what we put our faith into. If we read the Bible our faith in God will grow and we will begin to see mountains fall at our feet from our confession of faith. "So then faith comes by hearing, and hearing by the word of God. Romans 10:17 (KJV) Some people put their faith in people but they will end up failing us leaving us wounded. If we put our faith in fear then fear will lead us and we will be afraid.

Anne had fed the curse of death over her son until she was sick from worry. The medium inserted the seed into her mind, and Anne kept it growing through her believing it. The problem was she did not know how to get rid of the fear that was plaguing her. That was until she became a Christian, and saw in the Bible where she could break all curses, through the blood of Jesus. Then she was able to let it go from her thoughts.

It was years later when her son was traveling on a road that he had an accident. The truck in front of him was carrying long planks of wood in the back of the trailer that he was pulling. They were traveling pretty fast when the truck came to an abrupt stop; causing her son to slam on his brakes and clip the back end of the trailer. This caused the planks of wood to fly out off the back of the trailer at lightning speed. They flew through the air and came through her son's windshield like a torpedo, pinning him to his seat! When the rescue workers and his mother arrived on the scene of the accident, they saw a huge plank of wood one centimeter from her son's throat. When Anne saw her son she fell on her face crying, thanking God because she knew Jesus had broken the demonic curse put on her son years earlier. This shows us the mighty power of faith in Jesus over the enemy's lies!

In the atmosphere above our heads, there is a battle between angels and demons for our souls. Which one will win? If the price has already been paid for our soul, by Jesus's death, then why is there still a battle for us? Because God gave us a choice! He wants us to believe in Him and love Him because we love Him, not because we are forced to. The devil on the other hand hates us more than we know, and also HATES God with a passion. His ultimate goal is to be God, and he uses us to accomplish this.

It is like a game of tug-of-war. Jesus is on one side with two thirds of the angels while on the other side is Lucifer with one third of his devils and demons, and they are playing for your soul. Satan needs you to get on his side to help him win. Isaiah 4 tells us that because of the wickedness, hell's doors are widening themselves to receive all the people that are choosing his side.

This tells us that it is NOT God that sends us to hell, but we ourselves that make that choice. God does not want robots forcing people to love him. No, He waits patiently for us to respond, in hopes that we will choose life. Sadly, many cannot see Satan's evil plan, because of this blindness that he puts on our minds; people then jump on his side, denying the God who patiently waits for them. Although God made them, they rejected him in "He was in the world, and though the world was made through him, the world did not recognize him. He came to that which was his own, but his own did not receive him. Yet to all who did receive him, to those who believed in his name, he gave the right to become children of

God children born not of natural descent, nor of human decision or a husband's will, but born of God." 1 John 1:13

If the devil can get our minds on anything but Jesus, he will steal our birthrights to heaven. He slowly puts us to sleep, and then we start moving toward the gas chambers, unaware of his devices. Tolerance of sin is the number one cyanide pill that he slips to us. We have an enemy that hates us!

"Rescue those, by snatching them from the flames, but do so with great caution, hating the sins that contaminate their lives." Jude 22:23. Notice that it does not say hate the person in the flames, but the SINS that contaminate their lives! We don't like what the effects of alcohol do to a love one. We wrench in pain from the effects of what drugs do to destroy a friend. We hate what happens when a spouse is unfaithful, and we DESPISE abuse! In other words: I may hate what you do, but I truly LOVE you!

I once met a woman, who said she went to church but kept quietly to herself, as she didn't want to offend or ruffle anyone's feathers by counseling them to do right. So I asked her, "If your neighbor's house was on fire and you could see that there were children in the upstairs window, would you not run over there in a panic, pounding on the door screaming, "FIRE! Get out!?" Wouldn't you do everything you could to rescue any and all of those in the house? I could not believe her answer: she said, "No, because I might get burnt and get overcome by the fire myself! I would probably wait for the fire department to come." Frustrated I said, "But what if there was no time, and you could hear the people crying for help. Would you not get a ladder or something?" Then she said, "No, I would have to pull my blinds, so I could not see them or hear their screams and wait for the firemen."

I stood in wonderment, and I could not help but think, "Is this how Christians (children of God) feel?" I had a deep grieving feeling in my spirit, and said, "What ever happened to the scripture, 'LOVE your neighbor as YOURSELF'? She shrugged her shoulders and said, "I just don't want to get burnt." I then went to get into my car, but turned and said, "I sure hope you are never "Your" neighbor; with that I drove away.

"There is no greater love than to lay down one's life for one's friends." John 15:13. How many countless men and woman have there been through the years who have given their lives for us? They have lost their lives that we might live, that we might be FREE! And should I not mention "Christ" who gave up His life for us so that we could have eternal life? Because of this freedom that we have been given; should we not also try and rescue others from the flames?

33 - Addiction

We spent most of our time speaking on how to stay demon free. Simple: just don't sin! Yeah right!

Seriously, these people who had demons were CHURCH PEOPLE, people who believed in God, and wanted to go to church, but kept on sinning!

Whenever we live anyway we want to rather than, how the bible says, we are in danger. 1 John 3 says, "The reason the Son of God appeared was to destroy the devil's work. No one who is born of God will continue to sin, because God's seed remains in them; they cannot go on sinning, because they have been born of God. This is how we know who the children of God are, and who the children of the devil are."

You might be saying, "But no one is perfect." You're right: no one is! So what does that scripture mean, that says, "No one who is born of God will continue to sin? God's seed remains in them; they cannot go on sinning?"

Good question; do you remember what that first love in your life felt like? Remember how you would light up when you saw them, tripping over your words and never wanting an argument to come between you two? Wouldn't you feel deep sorrow if you hurt them, apologizing extensively, because you wanted to fix the wrong as soon as possible. This apology closed the door to a wall trying to form between the two of you. It did not allow accusations to build up for future arguments. The small hurt was washed away from your wonderful relationship just by humbling yourself, apologizing and saying "I'm sorry."

The same is the case with our relationship with God. If we are His, then when and if we sin, we confess it immediately, bringing us back to that great relationship with Him. If we do not confess it, a wall starts to build up between us. We may ignore His gentle nudge and continue on our own way. This continuing of sin may open a door wide enough for the enemy to come in. We must close the door FAST, by asking forgiveness from God and the person we might have hurt in the process. Otherwise, the enemy may see the opened door and come into your house. Now when that happens an exterminator has to come in and remove the pesky pests that have found their way in. The key is, don't give the devil access! Close the door QUICKLY!

Some people have left the door swinging wide open, disregarding everything that God says, by continuing to sin, making it habitual. They believe in God, but pay no attention to His voice anymore; they have become callous to it.

How Addiction is formed

Suppose a man sees pornography online. He thinks it's just a glance, but now he has just cracked the door open. He can quickly turn and ask God to forgive him and the door would close, but...then the next day he is drawn away and enticed by his OWN desire to look again. He has now popped open the door wide enough to get a foot through. Still there is no repentance to God, who is watching him. Day three, he is swooned by fiery passion to look again, widening the gap of the door. Now Lions are in the grass outside, with saliva running down their fangs, seeking, hunting their prey. The man has no idea they are there, it seems harmless enough, no one's around. Then next day the apple is drawn to entice him, so he drifts back onto the web site. The evil around him eyes the open door, and then makes its move. Bam! In comes blood-thirsty demonic spirits, they have entered by the lust of his eye! Now his house is filled with lust, perversions, rape, lies, shame, and now he is addicted! Now he can't stop on his own! What to do?

That's where we come in. Walking down the street, we find this man and now he needs deliverance. It did not have to be this way, all it would have taken was for him to turn and walk away closing the door behind him by asking God to forgive him at first glance, and he would be FREE!

This is what it means in Genesis 4:7 when Cain was contemplating on killing his brother. God tells Cain "sin is crouching at your door, it desires to have you, but 'You' must master it! "Once that sin entered into the mind the battle began. Capture your thoughts! Bring them down by your sword! Take it off the shelf, blow the dust off and take it out of its sheath!

34 ~ Windows of the Soul

When we left off with Cary he was leaving the courtyard late one night after an intense spiritual battle. I had known Cary for quite some time by now. He had been a very young boy when I first met him several years before, when I first started going to this island, It is wild how fast time flies, for he had now become a man. He had asked God to come into his life when he was very young, but he did not serve Him very long before he quickly fell away, because peer pressure pushed him to the limit, so he gave in under the weight of it. He left the ways of the Bible that he was raised up in and started to take on the ways of those around him, just to be accepted. Because of these bad choices, he quickly escalated toward being the leader of the pack, and because of this darkness entered him, but he had no idea that it had. He stopped going to church because he was under such conviction from The Holy Spirit every time he tried.

Something inside of him was getting all stirred up the night we saw him in the courtyard and it was driving him to go to the church. This reminds me of the year there was a blackout in New York City. There were no lights in the whole city except one lone street light. What was amazing about this was that this one street light attracted a crowd of people; however, every moth and bug in a ten mile radius was also driven to the light.

When he came in we could immediately see demons come up into his eyes. Cary dropped to the floor screaming, because God was now in his house! There was definitely a Clashing of two Swords going on in the inside of him. God's presence was like a giant flashlight that, and had just been turned on in a dark room. It's just like a how a moth is driven to a lamp inside a house to swirl around it, compelled to stay at the light even though a slapping hand tries to end its flight. These demon spirits were doing the same thing; they were driven to the church but scrambling to get away from us, because of God's light in our eyes. The Bible says, in Matthew 6:22 "The eye is the lamp of the body. If your eyes are good, your whole body will be full of light. But if your eyes are bad, your whole body will be full of darkness. If then the light within you is darkness, how great is that darkness!" So in a sense the eyes of a person are the windows of their soul, and we could see darkness rising up in their windows!

Cary's face was totally distorted, because the demons in him were moving him wildly. It was almost as if he had autism or something like it. The demons knew that we were there to cast them out, but it was clear that they did not want to go! However, that was not an option: they had to bow to God's almighty presence. We knew that Cary had demons and that they were very strong. The night that we tried to cast them out of Todd, they also manifested in Cary, but as a venomous snake striking at our heels. Remember all the familiar spirits in that neighborhood? They were drawn out like magnets to gather around the courtyard to give the high arch ruler and the strongman fuel, because he was in trouble.

Cary was playing the part of the harlot. The enemy's purpose through the strategy of harlotry is to draw God's people away from faithful relationship with God. The enemy uses the enticements of the world to activate the lust of the flesh, of the eyes, and the pride of life. Cary's heart then turns to respond to the seduction. Hosea 4 says this very thing: "For a spirit of harlotry has led them astray, and they have played the harlot, departing from their God"

A Proverb tells Cary's story as follows:

"'The temptress, she is a smooth talking, Seductress, for she will lead you away as an adulteress with her sly flattering words pierce slowly into a heart.

"I once was at the window of my house when I looked out through the lattice; through my curtains and saw a foolish, simpleminded; naive, young man, he was just a boy. I noticed he had no wisdom, no sense to know the difference from right from wrong. I saw him walking down the street near the corner, and then he crossed the street, near the house of an immoral woman, just strolling down the street when he then took the pathway to her house.

It was at twilight, in the evening, as deep darkness fell. There she was, dressed like a prostitute. She approached him; she propositioned him, for she was hungry for love, for a victim.

She was, boisterous and loud, filled with pride and very defiant. I was surprised that she was there, for she never stayed at home. You always saw her out in the streets or in the city squares, just standing around, lurking on the street corners.

Before he knew what was happening to him, caught unaware in the trap in front of him. She grabbed him and kissed him passionately. Without any shame she said to him, "I go to church, for I am a good person, and I keep promises that I make." Then with deep seduction in her eyes she whispers, "I have been looking for you, I have been seeking your face and now I have found you."

Then winking she leans forward and under her breath she says, "I have covered my bed with colored satin sheets from Egypt. Yes, just for you, I have just changed my linens and sprinkled my bed with the sweetest most exotic smelling perfumes. Come with me, let's become intoxicated with love until morning. Come, let's caress in each other's arms and enjoy each other's love, for my husband is not home; he has gone on a long overseas trip. He had a huge business deal and so he took a lot of money with him. Don't worry he will be gone for a long time.

By the flattery of her lips she seduces him; by her enticing words she melts him to butter. Right then, an arrow shot through his liver, as I watched him, he was star struck, love-sick, and foolishly followed her to her den. He was like an ox led to the slaughter, or a bird caught in a net with no way out. The black widow spider had created a huge web that most could not see. But once the webbing

127

caught her food, she ran to the center to surround her prey in a silky bed, before enjoying her feast.

He did not realize that it would cost him his life.

The spirit of harlotry is not passive but very aggressive and it starts from early childhood, to build a "secret life. Cary also was trapped as a young boy. It is amazing how accurate the words of the Bible are, because in Proverbs 6 it says "An adulteress, hunts for a precious life." It is evil how the enemy hunts for us like an animal.

Cary had been involved in leading up a campaign to destroy the foundation of the church, by way of rebellion. The Bible tells us that rebellion is the same as witchcraft. The seducing spirit also became very perverted and sexual. He brought everyone that he came in contact with into this mighty web of destruction. This in time, made him (or the demonic) stronger and stronger, until it became a stronghold of iron in this community!

"Have nothing to do with the fruitless deeds of darkness, but rather expose them. For it is shameful even to mention what the disobedient do in secret. But everything exposed by the light becomes visible—and everything that is illuminated becomes a light." Ephesians 5:11

Amazingly, before we arrived at the church, God revealed to us through an email what kind of demonic force we would come in contact with, and what its name was. Its name was PRIDE!

Pride is a huge spirit normally, but what we would find in Cary was far from normal, no, it had grown into a monstrous Godzilla. It had deep roots and, like the Hindu gods, a massive amount of arms and legs, all going in different directions.

Cary would growl like a rabid dog, as spirit after spirit came up and out of him. He was filled with shame, unworthiness, fear, self-hatred, un-forgiveness, and all the more.

As each spirit left him, he stood taller and taller and even started talking sensibly, but there was still one demon left, for we could see it appear in Cary's eyes. This demon was somehow being controlled by something or someone in the corner of the church rafters. Cary's eyes were literally fixed; it was like he was mesmerized. He cocked his head slightly as if he was receiving instructions. I looked up to see if there was something there, for he made it so convincing that something was up there by his staring and head turning. I could not see anything with my natural eye, but my spiritual eye was telling me to turn him around so that whatever it was that was controlling him could not communicate with him anymore. It worked!

I had quickly remembered a dream that a young girl from church had just had. It had involved green monster spirits with arms of different lengths, in the church rafters. I did not want to take any chances about what was subconscious or what was real. Things around there were just plain weird!

I started binding different strong men but no response came from the demon, and then finally I remembered my email. That's when I said, "I bind the strong man of pride. BINGO! I got a response! He threw his head back and straightened up his face as if he was puffed up and proud! I said, "Ah huh, I know who you are now, you serpent!" He then squinched in his nose, showed his teeth and snarled at me like a rabid dog. I knew it was the master spirit of PRIDE! Haughty and arrogant it fought us, until finally he gave a big scream and it came out of him! Fewwwy...

Todd came up to Cary and said, "Cary, I break covenant with you, all soul ties I have made with you, and I ask you to forgive me." Todd then wrote on a piece of paper with his name on one side and Cary's on the other and ripped it into two pieces. He was signifying to the devil that this relationship was severed. Then he and Cary prayed to God and asked Him to forgive them for becoming entangled in sin's web. Both of the men were crying for joy, as they both said that they felt completely free! Then Cary went one by one to all of those he had influenced to sin and asked them for forgiveness as well. Everyone was in tears, as bondage after bondage lay broken on the church floor. Cary's family was so excited by the difference in him that they invited all of us to a dinner of celebration!

Cary was so different that my words come up empty. I cannot begin to tell it like it really happened. This precious guy felt totally unworthy; he hung his head, feeling like nothing more than dirt on the ground. What a liar the devil is! Cary walked all slumped over from the chains that the enemy had on him, but, when God reached out his hand to Cary, not to beat him down but to lift him up and call him "Son." Every shameful thought plaguing his mind came crashing down to the floor and vanished under the powerful hand of Love.

"The Love of God, who can measure it? Neither death nor life, nor angels nor demons nor principalities nor powers, nor things present nor things to come, neither height nor depth, nor any other created thing, shall be able to separate us from the love of God which is in Christ Jesus our Lord!" Now that's good news!

35 - An Earthquake

The mountain was our next destination, but before I tell you about this trip I am reminded of a previous trip up this mountain. It was much like a trip to the underground. It was just a few years back, and it left an imprint on my memory that I will never forget. Jean and I were exhausted, but we got on board a big bus going up the mountain. We chose a seat about mid-way back and sat down thinking we would catch a nap, as the ride was to be about four hours long. Others were still boarding when a troop of shady looking creatures came aboard. We were told they were Gypsies. There were probably ten of them and when they got on they scattered all over the bus. Several of them headed to the back of the bus, a few got behind Jean and me and two got in front of us. They had no manners, absolutely no morals and NO shame!

The bus driver started to go, and when we had been traveling for about ten minutes the two in front of us turned around and looked right at us. It was very awkward, but we smiled at them to be polite, thinking that would help. Neither of them had brushed their hair or their teeth in what appeared to be a couple of years, and now they were directly staring at us, breathing through their dragon breath filled mouths.

One was chewing tobacco wildly and then spitting into a can, missing most of the time so it splattered on the seat and floor beside him. The other one was now staring intently at our purses, with no reserve. We both grabbed our bags and sat on them, for we had heard that gypsies are extremely fast pick pockets and your money and valuables disappear before your eyes. Behind us four of them were down on the floor doing something. All of a sudden there was a horrendous smell coming from their contaminated back seat. I won't for (for the sake of a G rating) go into what they were doing, but will tell you that they all needed a jail cell.

Jean and I started to pray and bind this lewd behavior, and pray for protection over us, because the bus driver was now flying down the other side of the mountain at horrendous speeds. We literally had to hold on to the seat in front of us because he was going so fast. On a few occasions I felt sure we were only riding on two wheels. I was petrified, for it appeared as if the same spirit of the Gypsies had gotten into him too.

When we turned around the other gypsies were laughing and mocking their immoral behavior. Now the guys in the front of the bus started to respond to them, shouting back and forth in their language to each other. All the while they were spitting green slime from their teeth as they shouted.

One of them in the front had asked the bus driver to play a filthy raunchy movie on the DVR that they had brought with them. It was so loud and blaring obscenities while all of this nauseating behavior was going on in the back of the bus. Jean and I were so upset we looked for another seat (as if that would help any) but they were all filled. The two in front of us were now poking at our seats, taunting us by trying to get our purses; I was livid. I would have decked both of them, but in a second eight more would have instantly been on top of me. There appeared to be no way out, but up!

I looked at Jean and said, "Let's sing!" and she said, "OK!" So we sang, "There is POWER, POWER, Wonder Working POWER, in the BLOOD of the Lamb! There is POWER, POWER Wonder Working POWER in the Precious BLOOD of the Lamb!" We sang and we sang! We even sang verses that we made up on our own. We sang for twenty minutes all about the blood of Jesus. Do you know what happened next? You will not believe it! God put them all asleep: every last one of them dozed off like babies and never woke up again until we got there! Some even snored, but that was all right with us.

Miraculously, the bus driver slowed the bus down and turned the movie off! It was a miracle! There's definitely Power in The BLOOD of JESUS! Gypsies, Tramps and Thieves; Cher was right when she made that song!

Now, you can say, maybe it was our horrendous singing voices that put them to sleep. Whatever works, God did it! Oh Yeah...

Some people came and told Jehoshaphat, "A vast army is coming against you from the other side of the Dead Sea. Alarmed and in fear, Jehoshaphat prayed to the Lord; Then Jehoshaphat prayed 'We cry out to you in our distress, and you will hear us and save us. For we have no power to face this vast army that is attacking us. We do not know what to do, but our eyes are on you."

A prophet rose up and said, "This is what the Lord says to you: You will not have to fight this battle. Take up your positions; stand firm and see the deliverance the Lord will give you. Do not be afraid; do not be discouraged. Early in the morning Jehoshaphat appointed men to sing to the Lord and to praise him for the splendor of his holiness as they went out at the head of the army, singing: "Give thanks to the Lord, for his love endures forever."

As they began to sing and praise, the Lord set ambushes against the men and they were defeated. Jehoshaphat and all the men returned joyfully to Jerusalem, for the Lord had given them cause to rejoice over their enemies." 2 Chronicles 20:27

God protected David by putting Saul into a deep sleep when he was chasing David to kill him. "David took the spear and water jug near Saul's head, and they left. No one saw or knew about it, nor did anyone wake up. They were all sleeping, because the Lord had put them into a deep sleep." 1 Samuel 26:12

Ok, now back to the beginning. We are on this incredible four hour bus ride to get to this mountain city and God was right there with us too! Anne and I were sharing a seat together talking about all that God had just done in the church and just how incredible He actually is. We both had our Bibles open, but amazingly we were both on the same page. The very scripture that we were both reading was about Jesus talking about "A Mountain."

Isaiah 64:3 says "Come down to make your name known to your enemies and cause the nations to quake before you." I was thinking, "We are traveling up a mountain, so the only thing missing was an earthquake." I kept reading, "When you did awesome things that we did not expect, you came down, and the mountains trembled before you." Okay, well that was true too. He had done incredible things but seriously was He actually speaking to us? Now, this had our attention, the Bible was speaking to us as if it were a person? In the book of Hebrews it says that it is Alive, and to us it was, for it leaped off the page of the book and spoke to us as if we were having a cup of coffee with a friend.

As we whirled and twirled through the mountains we could see smoke rising from the ground. We were so high that we could actually touch the clouds as we went up. The bus driver would swerve around a curve going way too fast and everyone on the bus would gasp. There were no guard rails protecting you from going over the edge at any given moment and it was an extremely long way down. The driver paid no attention to signs all along the way that said "Slow very steep" and "Look out for falling rocks below." Many rockslides had claimed lives every year and the crosses and flowers along the roadside had indicated that some were quite recent. The road up was so very steep and narrow that there was not an inch of breathing room. Crazy people (probably from the USA) would try to pass each other on this narrow itty bitty roadway and so fall over the edge to their death. Hmm... Matthew 7 says "Make every effort to enter through the narrow door, because many, I tell you, will try to enter and will not be able to. For wide is the gate and broad is the road that leads to destruction, and many enter through it. But small is the gate and narrow the road that leads to life and only a few find it."

Finally we made it to our destination, but we had to cross a narrow three foot wood plank bridge over a huge ravine of water. One thing I was thankful for was that we were not there at night or in the rain, for it was extremely steep and very slippery. The people came running because they were so happy to see us make it up the eighty eight steep stairs. I felt like I rewrote the song "Over the River and through the woods" to "Over the mountain and through the mud, walk on the plank, scale the steps and to the top of the world we go" The scripture kept going through my mind "If you build your house on the sand it will surely fall." The muddy mountain side was the very walls in their homes.

Huffing and puffing we made it to the mountain people's Bible study. These precious people started a Bible study immediately after a major mud slide had taken place. One dark night a horrendous typhoon rose up while they slept and tore through the mountain side. The rain was so fierce that night that it caused a massive mud slide and took over three hundred lives as their houses, cars and families just slid away, never to be seen again. The stories that we heard from the people were completely devastating in every way, for most had at least someone, if not the whole family, dead. The enemy took total advantage of their losses and started showing many of them ghostly images. A lot of them were hearing voices coming up from the ground up to three weeks after the mud slide had taken place. Although they missed their loved ones, they were terrified by these voices and ghostly images that would appear as the sun would go down. This caused a lot of questions to pop up concerning spiritual things and they were in need of some serious answers.

I was truly amazed as for most of the people did not blame God for their losses, but they blamed Satan and rightly so for he did it! There are times when people blame God when a disaster happens, when in reality the enemy is to blame. Some might say, "Well God does allow it to happen, right?" Well let's see...

"Jesus says, "There were eighteen on whom The Tower in Siloam fell and killed them, do you think that they were worse sinners than all other men who dwelt in Jerusalem? I tell you, no; but unless you repent you will all likewise perish." (Luke 13:4) Jesus told them this story so that they would repent and not be like these people that died. He was also talking about a Barren Fig Tree when He says, "A certain man had a fig tree planted in his vineyard, and he came seeking fruit on it and found none. Then he said to the keeper of his vineyard, 'Look, for three years I have come seeking fruit on this fig tree and find none. Cut it down; why does it use up the ground?' But he answered and said to him, 'Sir, let it alone this year also, until I dig around it and fertilize it. And if it bears fruit, well. But if not, after that you can cut it down.'"

The bottom line is this: some very good and even godly people die in disasters, right along with someone who has rejected Jesus all their lives. Jesus knows who will come and who will NOT come to Him in this lifetime. He is patient that none should perish or die without Him, but the time comes when the door of patience is shut. If people do die in a disaster somewhere, God did not terminate them, but they terminated themselves by their refusal to repent.

Everyone knows that tax day is April 15th, right? Now some do their taxes early and get a refund. Others procrastinate and find the deadline upon them with no time to prepare. Still others have to get an extended grace period. Regardless of the situation, EVERYONE MUST do their taxes and they all know the date to have them done by. When the big day comes, April 15th, the time of grace has ended. If we have not gotten them done on time it is no one's fault but our own. We had all year to do them or another way of looking at it is: We have all our lives with countless opportunities to get right with God and now time is up! "The axe is already at the foot of the tree." Matthew 3:10

We cannot blame anyone but ourselves in the end. Neither the government nor God is to blame; however there is one we might blame.

God says, "Adam where are you?" Adam comes out of hiding holding a maple leaf around him and says, "Here I am, I was scared because I am naked!" Then God says, "Who told you that you are naked?" He says, "Ah. Um... Lord it was the woman YOU gave me!" So God looks at the woman, and she says, "Look, it wasn't me, I didn't do it! It was the snake! So God looks at the snake and the snake says, "Ah... I was just doing what I do best, deception!"

Back to the mountain people, they listened with open hearts because they definitely realized that what they were going through was not human. It was of a spiritual level that they were not familiar with so they needed heaven's attention.

There was one Muslim guy there that came with some friends because he too was hearing voices. He listened to the message that was all about Jesus being the Only Way to heaven. He had told his friends that his shoulder was hurting him really bad, and so his friends had convinced him to get us to pray for it, so we prayed for him. After the prayer he moved his shoulder full circle and to his amazement there was No Pain, for God had healed him! That's when he and all that were with him gave their lives to Christ. The whole house was amazed! It blew him away that even though he did not believe, God had healed him.

We had no idea of what our night was going to entail but I guess the enemy was hot on our trail to the house. We were told that whenever anyone visited the mountain people there would be a serious satanic attack after they returned. Really? Gulp… "Are you serious? A spiritual attack, you have got to be kidding me! Well nothing could have scared me as bad as that terrifying bus ride up the mountain did, I don't think. Double gulp…Does anyone have a barf bag? I feel sick!"

Okay, so far so good, we walked the plank back to civilization and managed to get off the mud slide mountain and back to our hotel. When we got back, we were staying on the third floor of a very nice hotel in the middle of the city. Everyone was exhausted so we knew sleep was going to come easy, or so we thought!

It was around midnight, and I am sure there was a full moon out, when all of a sudden Jean started shaking violently. She woke the whole room where we were all sleeping due to her unusual behavior. We started putting all of our blankets on top of Jean as she was trembling from the inside out. Just then, out of nowhere Marie screamed and was jarred to her feet dancing, because of a horrible leg cramp. As Marie groaned in agony from the muscle cramp in her leg, her other leg got one too!

When things could not have gotten any worse, they did. A huge flying roach flew across the room just missing Lynn's head, and then another, and another all at the same time. I went to turn on the light but it would not work. I tried and tried but it just would not turn on for anything, so the only light we had was that which was coming through the window. We managed to locate the humongous roaches and killed all of them, but just as the last one was dying, a massive pack of wild savage dogs started snarling and growling outside of our window below. They came out of nowhere, but they were extremely loud and sounded like they were tearing apart an animal of some kind. This was so strange for we could not even believe this was happening to us! Anne and I picked up our Bibles and started using them as SWORDS as we prayed, for we knew what was going on. Someone was not happy with what had gone on that night on top of that mountain. We had aroused a sleeping giant! Satan thought that mountain was his domain but we walked up that mountain as an army, all holding lamps just like Joshua in the Bible. We broke our lamps at the battle cry and watched as the "walls of the enemy's lies" all came crashing down!

Anne and I stood next to the window holding our Bibles out like SWORDS commanding evil of every kind to leave. Everything in the hotel room had calmed down. Jean was sleeping soundly with no shaking, all the bugs had been killed off and the muscle cramps in Marie's legs had loosened. There were now two deep rays of light shooting through the window and remaining on the wall of our room. We could not figure out where they were coming from but we knew somehow that they were help from heaven. That's when the pack of wild dogs started to move, and the more we prayed the further away they moved. Here is the interesting thing: we were stone tired, leaning against the wall, and holding out our Bibles, but as soon as we went to put them down the dogs got closer. We could definitely feel that satanic forces were fighting God's angels. Swords really were clashing on that night. As for Anne and me, we felt like Aaron and Moses on the mountain.

"As long as Moses held up the staff in his hand, the Israelites had the advantage. But whenever he dropped his hand, the Amalekites gained the advantage. Moses' arms soon became so tired he could no longer hold them up. So Aaron and Hur found a stone for him to sit on. Then they stood on each side of Moses, holding up his hands. So his hands held steady until sunset." Exodus 17:8-12. Anne and I did this until sunrise, wow what a night! Now, what's tomorrow going to bring?

When the time came for our descent, to my great surprise the mountain did start to shake! When we were getting ready to leave, we were standing outside waiting for a cab to come and pick us up, when the whole ground started shaking. I thought to myself, "Was this my imagination?" I said to the others, "Did you feel that?" Then sirens started going off around the city and some kids ran by us and yelled, "Did you feel the earthquake?" I said, "I think so, wait, did you say Earthquake?" They responded, "Yes, we've just had five mini-earthquakes in the last thirty minutes. They say that they are registering at 5.4 on the Richter scale. Also they're saying that they are expecting a big one, in about an hour!" Just then our cab pulled up and we boarded with lightning speed. We wanted to get off the mountain before the big one came, because they are known for rock slides.

I could not help being blown away by God speaking directly to us about this particular trip. The Bible that we had opened up spoke specifically to us and said, "Renee and Anne listen to me and I will unveil the secrets of the scriptures to you." Those who search for me will find me and I will make myself known to them." (Proverbs 8:17) How were we to keep this kind of thing quiet? Who would believe it, knowing that the God of the universe spoke to us, who are we anyways? Just whosoevers...

36 - Entry Points

I hope this answers some of the questions that you may be having.

I would have no idea as of what I was talking about, when it comes to deliverance or self-deliverance by the Blood of Jesus, but the Holy Spirit has shed a lot of light on this subject and He has shared with us through scriptures and experiences.

Have you ever heard a story on the news that told of the progressive development of the behavior of a man who murdered his girlfriend? First you might hear that this man was jealous of her friends and her talking to men. That might have progressed into suspicion or accusation, which leads into anger. If he does not handle the anger it can develop into rage and then ultimately to murder. He could have stopped it all along the way, but he probably never knew it would have been taken that far. The stronghold was taking effect with each progression of his behavior. Can you see how the enemy works by stalking us? He even sets us up, because he knows how predictable we are.

There is a healthy form of jealousy that causes us to step it up a bit. Say that on your job you have been really slack and someone in the office ends up getting a promotion that you have wanted. Jealousy may play a part in getting you motivated to step up your work ethics. But one must be careful not to become possessive or jealous to the point of revenge, for anything taken to the extreme can become a dangerous playground.

Suspicion is also not bad to a small degree; we need it when we suspect evil or if something appears to be wrong. But if it rules us and we become suspicious of everything and everyone around us, it has gone too far.

Also, God's word says that it's okay to be angry; we just can't dwell on it, sleep on it, or act on it. We must forgive whoever made us mad and let it go; the Bible say just don't sin in your anger. If you must go get a stone from the yard, go out to a field to an abandoned glass house and throw it. Busting the glass instead of what's in your house helps you to let things go. Rage however is wrong: it's very serious and you need to get help immediately if you find yourself losing control to rage.

Check yourself; ask "Am I balanced"? Differing weights are strongholds waiting to happen.

I have a friend who is a licensed mental illness psychologist. She takes mentally ill people and councils them back to an everyday lifestyle, through a course of deep counseling and spiritual skills through a state ordinance. I said, "We do the same thing!" She stepped back and her eyebrows went up, then she blurted out, "You do? Where do you work?" I said, "Yes we do, but it's not through a job or through any organization, but by the power of God."

I then continued, "Say a woman has a problem with anger, when she gets really, really upset she loses control and it seems to go into rage. When we talk with this woman, we try to find out when she first noticed this out-of-control problem. It might go all the way back to her childhood. We locate the day that she got really angry and exploded, and then we take her back to that incident. It may have been when she was really hurt by a close relationship. It could be that her father had a bad temper, and would hit her mother, ultimately leading them to a horrible divorce. This woman might have blown up, and gone out of control on her father for his hurtful behavior. This was the entry point for anger to enter her life; because that anger is never dealt with, it festered like a boil and went into rage. After that, every time her father's name was mentioned by anyone, there was nothing but vile poison coming from her mouth toward him. She had nothing good to say, this kept the rage progressing, even entering her adult life, until it affected all of her relationships and she needed help!

We would then lead her through a prayer, to forgive her dad (this was key) for the terrible hurt that he had caused. Then we pray and apply the blood of Jesus to that day and or time period by washing it clean. We then have her renounce anger and rage in Jesus' name. She must declare to God that she does not want this evil thing living inside of her anymore. This then breaks the enemy's hold on her life from that point on. Rage and anger had a stronghold built up in her life, just through that one incident!

Once the stronghold is dealt with, we would command the enemy to let her go, for he was not welcome there anymore! He then HAS to leave, for his rights have just been shattered or taken away. This woman comes out the winner, she receives healing and deliverance to a life with no more anger or rage!"

My friend said, "Wow that is exactly what we do, we also trace the root of the problem back to their childhood, I'm amazed!" I said, "Yes, me too, it's all through the power of God, for He has given us wisdom, without the four years of credentials." She then said, "No it was eight years.

In theology verses experience, an experience filtered by the Bible always expels an argument. God showed me an interesting analogy just today.

I was letting my dog outside, as we were going to go on a ride together. I had put her in my car and ran back into the house to get my keys, when I noticed a huge spider web. It was stretched across the entry way of the door leading into the house. A very beautiful butterfly flew by my face and headed right toward the web. I screamed at it, "No don't go up there, you'll get stuck! There's a spider up there, just waiting to eat you." Of course the butterfly paid no attention to what I had to say and I watched as it got stuck anyway. It then started flapping its wings wildly, but this only thickened the web around it. I thought to myself, "Renee it's just nature, just let the spider enjoy its meal in peace." But because of the beauty of the butterfly it compelled me to fight for its freedom. I looked for the spider and saw it hiding in a slit on the house. It was huge and I saw it just watching and waiting as its victim the butterfly

143

was getting weaker and weaker by its struggle. I then noticed several other corpses of bugs that had not been as fortunate as the one I was getting ready to rescue. I looked for a branch, but found a long stick that I placed next to the butterfly so that it could attach itself to the stick and be rescued. When I brought the butterfly down to look at, I noticed that it was covered in webbing and still unable to fly. I held it up in my hands and gently removed the entire sticky web around its wings. Once the weight of the webbing was gone, it took to flight. It was set free from its prison of death and looked beautiful once again, flying up high in the sky. I got my keys out of the house and went back to my car smiling, for I thought, "He really is the God of deliverance!"

37 - Staying 𝓕𝓡𝓔𝓔

To stay clean, keep your feet washed!

"To Him who loved us, and washed us from our sins in His own blood." (Rev 1:50)

I hope you take a shower every day to remove all of the dirt, grime and sweat of this life off of you. That is what God's kingdom is like. If you say, "I have asked God to forgive me from my sins when I was young then great you just took a big shower with exfoliator and shampooed your hair. Still, you cannot expect that you will never sin again. Well, Jesus said in John 13:11 "Once you have had a bath you only need to wash your feet."(Humble yourselves). Once we have asked Jesus to forgive us of our sins initially, He erases all of them from His memory (in other words we shower). But in future days we only need to wash our feet from walking on the dirt of this world (or sinning every day). We strive for perfection, to not sin, but it won't happen, for no one is perfect. We must wash our feet daily if needed by Jesus' Blood. This however does not mean that we try to sin on purpose.

I see it like a dance performance; let's say we have a dancer who is in competition to win gold or perfection. The scale is one to ten, one being the lowest and ten being perfection. The dancer would never go out on stage saying in her heart, "I sure hope I get a three tonight." No, she would never say that, she would say, "I hope I can get the gold tonight, I am trying for a perfect ten." It's the same with Gods kingdom; we don't say, "I just offended them. Oh well, I just can't help myself, my mouth always gets me in trouble, it's just the way I was brought up." That is like saying all I want is a three score. No, we strive for the ten of perfection by taking up a cross on our shoulders like Christ and killing our flesh to achieve a higher score.

I knew a woman who had a sixteen year old son that she loved with everything in her. One deep dark night he was going way too fast and drove his car into a tree. He was killed on impact, but he was not the only one who died that night: it also killed her. Her spirit died with him on that night; his death destroyed her inside, because he was her only child. Her death affected her husband and all her friends, because she went into a deep dark depression state. She mourned, and mourned and mourned; for fifteen years she mourned. The Bible says there is set amount of time to mourn over a loved one, otherwise it is unhealthy and allows the devil to come in, through the grief. The enemy told her that God killed her son and that He does not care. He also told her that God is unfair and is the one to blame for his death because he could have stopped it!

She became a manic depressive and became suicidal as well. Then she started taking meds to calm her nerves down, but it only led to other meds that worsened the darkness inside her. She set up a shrine that she could mourn over, in the entryway of her home. She had all his photos from birth to high school. She also took all his awards and trophy's from games that he had played in and put them there too. There is nothing wrong with memories but when you make a home inside yourself and set up a person as an idol, the enemy is the one handing you the tools to build with. The second commandment says, "You shall not make for yourself a carved image, or any likeness of anything that is in heaven above, or that is in the earth beneath, or that is in the water under the earth; you shall not bow down to them nor serve them. For I, the LORD your God, am a jealous God"

When we found her, and saw her shrine, we took her all the way back to the night of her son's death, for this was the entry point of where the enemy came in to steal her life. It is absolutely wrong how he is able to do this to a person, but he waits and watches for an opportunity and pounces on it. We prayed with her about that night, she just wailed and wailed. She forgave God, for she blamed Him for taking her son out of her life.

When she gave birth to her son, she never dedicated him to God for His use. She made him an idol instead, and started to worship him. He could not move without his mother being right beside him in everything he did, so when it came time for her son to leave this world, she could not release him. It literally tore her apart inside and then she blamed God for doing it. The devil jumped on this! That night The Holy Spirit gently got her to see that her son was a precious gift from God, and He had entrusted her to raise him. He also told her that He was not the one who killed her son, but it was the enemy. God is the author of life, it's the enemy who comes to steal, kill and destroy our lives. In this case, he was not out to destroy just one life, but two.

She finally accepted the fact that He was NOT to blame; it was the enemy that took her son that night. She ended up believing God and turned the blame over to the enemy. That's when she smiled; she started to believe that her son was not dead like the enemy had told her. He had convinced her that her son was dead, but she had learned that she would see him again someday. That's when she tore down the shrine for she did not need it anymore, as she was left with a powerful memory in her mind of her son's life here on earth. That's how she sees him now, as part of the living, not the dead! She now lives free, helping others who can't see the devil's evil lies.

Let's say a little girl who is five years old gets raped by her uncle. A demon, or, for the sake of fear we will call them strongholds, may very possibly enter this poor little girl through this demonized man. Although the five year old is innocent of this abuse she is now a victim. We have seen it happen over and over again. The enemy wants to keep people in lifelong programs and on stress and anxiety meds. God wants to turn them around by using this incident as a stepping stone to help someone else out of a similar situation. Genesis 50:20 says "You meant evil against me; but God meant it for good, in order to bring it about as it is this day, to save many people."

Then the little girl starts to grow up, being so young she had suppressed the sexual abuse done to her, but she notices that she hates men. She tells everyone around her that she hates them and they are worthless. A word curse is being placed on her to HATE men, for Proverbs 18:21 says "The tongue has the power of life and death, and those who love it will eat its fruit." Now the enemy is beginning the process of stealing her life, for she may now become attracted to women because men repulse her. This would be another lying demon coming into steal her true identity. Leviticus 20:13 says "If a man has sexual relations with a man as one does with a woman; both of them have done what is detestable to the Lord." Also 1 Corinthians 6:8 says "Do not be deceived: Neither the sexually immoral nor idolaters nor adulterers nor men who have sex with men nor thieves nor the greedy nor drunkards nor slanderers nor swindlers will inherit the kingdom of God." She may become bitter with people of authority, especially with men. She may even become depressed or suicidal from other demonic spirits that have attached themselves through low self-esteem. This was all done to utterly destroy her. She now may have to see a counselor or go through years of therapy. What a mess, all because her uncle raped her! It was not even her fault! She now needs a miracle of healing and forgiveness that. If the strongholds don't leave when she gets saved, then she might be in need of deliverance.

We have seen all of these problems that the enemy does to someone, but we have also seen them totally set free by God's mighty deliverance power too. It is horrible what the enemy does to steal, kill and destroy us. Most of us have no knowledge of what the Bible says, for we let the church tell us what it says. God has already provided the answers for us, but we never pick up our swords so we have no idea how to stay clean.

We got a call one day by a woman to come clean her house. When I asked her if they had cleaned it from time to time she responded by saying, "No, and I am ashamed to tell you that." Then she added, "It needs serious help." When we got there to give an estimate, we found that she was exactly right, for she was in desperate need of a fire hose! After that day long exhausting cleaning she set herself up on a biweekly renewal program. She said that she felt like a new woman; she could sleep better and felt happy. She also said that she never wanted to get her house out of control like that again! Now this is deliverance!

This is exactly what it is like to pray with someone who has never had a spiritual bath from God. They must first repent of their sins, (Salvation) then God starts the cleaning, (self- deliverance, or deliverance of a stronghold), and after that comes the (healing)! Ooo, I feel good!

Jesus came to destroy the works of the enemy. 1 John 3:7 says, "The devil has sinned from the beginning. For this purpose the Son of God was manifested, that He might destroy the works of the devil." Yahoo! There is Help!

38 - Relationship

"Cast all your anxiety on him because he cares for you." He is not religious, stiff, mean, or out to get us, no He is The Ruler, The Judge, The Intercessor who prays for you, He's compassionate, and patient waiting for us to believe in Him, not wanting anyone to die without Him in their lives. 1Peter 5:6

All God wanted to do when he made Adam, was to walk in the garden with Him. He longed for a relationship with him, for this is why He made him in the first place. He gave Adam rule over all the animals, but Adam wanted a female, because he was not satisfied with God alone. (Imagine that) However, God was longing for his companionship regardless of Adam's response. It was not until seven generations later that Enoch grabbed God's attention. He was so pleased with Enoch that God took him up to be with Him in heaven. Could it be that Enoch longed to know Him intimately; could he have walked through the Garden of Eden wondering, "Who is this God?" God started revealing his heart to Enoch, He started sharing with Him visions and dreams and mysteries, all because Enoch loved Him. Relationship is all God has desired for us, not rituals, rehearsed prayers, lamentations, do and don'ts. He only set up rules and regulations to keep us from harm to ourselves and from the unseen enemy lurking all around us.

Having a relationship with a spouse is the exact way that we should look at our relationship with God. God also sees it this way, because He calls us his bride. Now, the way a marriage should work is one thing, but how it currently works is totally another. Let's just say that the couple we are speaking of is madly in love with each other. The husband loves his wife unconditionally; he catches a whiff of her sweet perfume as she passes by him, leaving behind a beautiful aroma in the room and He will do anything she desires. The wife, in response to this deep love, respects Him to the fullest. In turn she will speak of him everywhere she goes and do anything and everything he requests of her.

Out of our deep love for someone, we will do all sorts of things for them, like cook, clean, iron, wash clothes, do yard work, work long hours, take care of the car and the list can go on and on. All of these things come out of an act of love that we have toward the ONE we love. It should not be out of duty or obligation, though some may feel this way now. Remember when your love was new and fresh and alive for one another? Stir up the flame.

This is actually how God loves us. Ephesians 5:25 says, "Husbands, love your wives, just as Christ loved the church and gave himself up for her (on the Cross) to make her holy, cleansing her by the washing with water through the word." He is your husband if you believe in Isaiah 54:5 it says "For your Maker is your husband, the Lord of hosts is His name; and the Holy One of Israel is your Redeemer, the God of the whole earth He is called." He also wants to give us the desires of our hearts. Psalms 37:5 says, "Take delight in the Lord, and he will give you the desires of your heart..."

It does not matter if we study the scriptures like the Scribes and Pharisees did, for it was all knowledge to them. They knew the law inside out, and it still made them very religious, which is a stench in Gods nostrils. He was not talking about knowledge alone; however He does want us to know His Word. Knowledge by itself is puffed up, it says in the Bible "We all possess knowledge, but knowledge puffs up while love builds us up." God is spirit and longs to know us by our spirits, not a religious denomination. Otherwise we become religious. We are in relationship with a mighty powerful God, who loves us all greatly.

39 - The Great Debate

You might be saying to yourselves, "How can a Christian believer have a demon?" Hmm...

There is a debate; it's over the word "Christian." Can a Christian have a demon or be possessed by the devil? The debate is against two theories, the first one being: They must NOT be a Christian, because how can God (light) and the devil (darkness) exist together in the same body? This theory leaves us thinking, if a believer per say, thinks they have a demon, they can't be a Christian. Theory two says that a "Christian" CAN have a demon. This is based on the fact that a believer in Christ can sin. By sinning and continuing in their sin, without repentance, they can or will open a door for the demonic to enter. This theory leaves us thinking, that if a believer in Christ falls into a sinful state they can get a demon.

Defining the word Christian

The Bible says that if we are in Christ we will not keep on sinning, meaning habitual sin, for we all sin, just about every day for something. If we fear and don't have faith in a circumstance, the Bible says it is sin. God knows that we will sin, even though we are living a "Christian" lifestyle. By being in relationship with Him allows us to ask Christ to forgive us every day. This constant washing (is like taking a daily shower) by His blood, and also the continual reading of His Word, cleanses us just from the filth of the world on a daily basis. This action keeps us protected from all temptations and evil all around us.

Habitual sin is walking out from under God's mighty umbrella of protection to go our own way by choice. This leaves us unprotected to the open air around us, allowing for the enemy's fiery missiles to attack us. We still believe in God but no longer walk under his protection, so demons have a right to come in. Does believing in God alone make us a Christian, or is it in doing what his Bible says, that makes us one?

In the Old Testament it says Abraham believed God and it was accredited to him as righteousness. He was righteous or a "Christian" just by believing. But there was no law, Bible, rules or regulations set in place yet; the Bible says each man did what he saw right in his own eyes to do. Once the law was laid down, God expected us to not just believe, like Abraham, but to also "obey" the law, or His Word. By loving him with our whole being, mind and strength, this is what makes us a Christian.

Check this out:

Mark 7:26 says, "A woman from a gentile nation came to Christ, fell on her face and begged Jesus to drive the demon out of her daughter. Jesus replies "First let the "children of Israel" eat all they want," he also told her, "For it is not right to take the "children's bread" and toss it to the dogs or gentiles."

Are your thoughts making your head swim? Several chapters later, Paul is instructed by the Holy Spirit to go to the gentiles with the message. They become grafted into a vine, giving them the same benefits Israel has as children, including "eating of the bread." A person must be a Child of God to receive the benefits. Are not His benefits "deliverance", healing and salvation? The unbelieving do not get these rights for they are "Bread" and they are for the children of God alone!

The BIG questions is whether believing in Christ alone and then doing what we want to is that what makes us a Christian, or is it a lifestyle of obedience to His Word, putting us in relationship with Him? Can a Christian wander away from what he believes? Can he open himself up to the enemy by a reckless lifestyle? Are they called "Christians" or have they sold their birthright? You be the judge! All I know is, when you see someone manifesting an evil spirit, by spitting, growling, and uttering blasphemies to God, you cast it out, and answer the doctrinal questionnaire later!

40 - The Why's

Jesus' teachings were to some very hard, but to others a walk of Holiness, not wanting to give the enemy a FOOTHOLD of any kind! Holiness is not a set of rules, well to some it may seem to be, but like I've said, if you're In LOVE, they're not rules, no, they're "I want to's."

If God's Holy Book has every answer to life's problems in it, if it really gives out dividends to whoever believes them, if it excels, promotes, prospers, interprets dreams, unravels mysteries, leaps off the page as if it's alive, breaks strongholds, heals the body of sicknesses and gives wisdom beyond scholars, then why, oh why, doesn't everybody in this world have it pinned to their clothing? Why aren't stores sold out of the book as fast as they get it in? Why are there not fights and wars breaking out everywhere with anyone who dares to take it from us? Why? Because we are in a spiritual battle, that's why! Satan does not care if we go to church! As long as we don't pick up that Bible he is good, because he knows if we do then we will find out who we are. He doesn't want us to know who we are when we become one of God's children or the authority that Jesus gave us over him. He keeps our Bibles hidden in our houses, because if we find out what it says, his kingdom will be destroyed.

He knows that he has no power over us, but we don't. If we do pick up a Bible he makes us sleepy, or distracts us or makes us busy. He despises Jesus and every single one of us.

Just think when was the last time you saw someone carry a Bible in the church? Yes, I said CHURCH? We have laid our swords on our shelves at home in hopes that an overhead projector has one for us to pick up. Our armor is in a heap in our back yard under some lawn chairs. We are not ready for war, well maybe with our neighbor but not with the enemy of our soul who is stalking us. Tolerance is now a frequent word in our vocabulary but we cannot quote a scripture by memory.

I was blowing my shofar in a graveyard of a small church in the area around where I live. I was trying to wake the dead up spiritually by using the picture of a graveyard, commanding the dead around me to wake up and live. This was a picture to remind me that we are all sleeping while the enemy is plotting our death and destruction. 1Thessalonians 5:6 says "Let us not sleep, as others do; but let us watch and be sober."

Put on the full armor of God, so that you can take your stand against the devil's schemes. (Ephesians 6:10) Then take up the shield of faith, with which you can extinguish all the flaming arrows of the evil one. But don't forget the Sword of the Spirit, which is the word of God.

We know that if people don't believe that "The god of this world has blinded the minds of them that do not believe; otherwise the light of the glorious gospel of Christ, who is the image of God, would shine unto them to make them see." 2 Corinthians 4:4

So let's believe!

41 - Watch

Remember, therefore, what you have received and heard; hang on to it tight, and repent. But if you do not wake up, I will come like a thief, and you will not know at what time I will come to you." Revelation 3:5

An air traffic controller in Nevada fell asleep early one morning as a medical flight carrying someone sick tried to land. Federal authorities ordered an immediate end to leaving just one controller on duty during an overnight shift.

Authorities said, "Air traffic controllers are responsible for making sure aircrafts safely reach their destinations. They reported that they cannot or will not tolerate sleeping on the job! This type of unprofessional behavior does not meet their high safety standards." They said that they would put an additional controller on the midnight shift for towers all around the country. Where there has previously only been one person manning the assigned position, now they would have two. The news followed several different reports of controllers sleeping on the job. One included a controller supervisor who supposedly dozed off while two planes landed. Miraculously they did not collide and no one was hurt this time, thanks be to God.

God speaks to us all the time through the things around us every day. When we turn on the news and hear that an air traffic controller, one who directs planes to safety, was sleeping, is that all we hear? Or can we look at the spiritual side of what He is saying? Jesus used everyday stories to show us spiritual truths, but we must listen with our spirit. I believe God is speaking to us about more than just a news story here. So what is he saying? I believe He is saying, "He who has an ear let him hear what the Holy Spirit says. Wake up! "Be on guard! Be alert! You do not know when the time will come."

Consider this; it's like a man going away: He leaves his house and puts his servants in charge, each with their assigned task, and tells the one at the door to keep watch. "Therefore keep watch because you do not know when the owner of the house will come back—whether in the evening, or at midnight, or when the rooster crows, or at dawn. If he comes suddenly, do not let him find you SLEEPING. What I say to you, I say to everyone: 'Watch!" Mark 13:36

42 - The Lamb!

God knows absolutely everything about you. He knows your actions: when you sit down and when you get up, when you go and when you return. He intimately knows all your ways. He knows your words: actually He even knows what you are going to say before you say it! He also knows your every thought from far away before they even get to you. He has you surrounded, with His hand upon you if you love Him. There is no escape from His eternal knowledge. In Psalms 139 King David says, "Such knowledge is too much for me to take in, it's is too high for me to grasp with my brain, I can't register it."

We think we know ourselves, but do we? Jeremiah 17:9 says, "The heart is more deceitful than all else and is desperately wicked; who can understand it?" We can't know our own motives unless God reveals them to us through His Word. God is the only one who knows us completely, through and through.

David asks the Lord "Where can I run to hide?" When Adam and Eve sinned they tried to hide from God so they sewed together, (who knows where they got the thread) fig leaves to hide their nakedness even from each other. (Genesis 2:25) It is a true fact that in the right setting, when a couple is married some have had a problem of exposing their bodies to their mates, so they make love in the dark. Some, or most, depending on the situation, fear being totally exposed. That goes for anything.

But the amazing thing is that this God who knows us so thoroughly, who knows every awful thought we ever have, desires to have a relationship with us. Because of our sin and God's holiness, something had to be done to remove that barrier to our relationship with Him. With the first couple, Adam and Eve, we see they made fig leaves but they could not hide from God the sin they committed. God slaughtered an animal and clothed them with its skin, showing them that they could not be reconciled to fellowship with Him, a holy God without the shedding of blood.

Although the Bible doesn't specify, can you imagine the first time as they watched the blood spurt from the animal who gave its life to cover their sin? It showed them in a very graphic way that God takes sin extremely seriously. It must be paid for through the taking of a life. It also showed them that in His great mercy, God would provide a solution so that no sinner had to be separated from God, or pay the penalty for their own sin.

Christianity is this way also; it is a personal relationship with the living God who knows you thoroughly. He brings you back into the same relationship that Adam had before he sinned. Actually, the Bible says that Jesus is the second Adam! "The first man Adam became a living being; the last Adam, a life-giving spirit. The spiritual did not come first, but the natural, and after that the spiritual. The first man was of the dust of the earth, the second man from heaven." 1Corinthians 15

God knew that blood from animals was not going to be able to cleanse you because they are under you. Their blood can cover your sins for a period of time but they cannot cleanse your sins. God told Adam to rule over them so how can their blood cleanse us? It was only a temporary fix, for God already knew that He was going to have to send His Son.

The people would bring the best and most spotless animal that they had to the priest every year. The reason that it had to be spotless is because it had to cover their sins. They didn't want to give the priest one with a broken leg or skin problem or even with spots all over it. No, it had to be the best looking one they had in their flock. I mean for heaven's sake this was to take away their sins, imagine some sins probably needed an extra big lamb! Oh yeah, it was so worth it!

The priest would then sacrifice the bulls, goats and lambs for the people's sins every year, but it only held good for them until they left the stage and sinned again. I'm sure you might have one lone soul that would leave the priest's presence, walk down the stairs and lust after some woman prostitute standing in the crowd. God knew that this was not going to do it, so He provided His very own Son to become a lamb! The lamb or Jesus had to be from heaven because Adam was made eternal when God formed him before his sin. He also had to be human because Adam was human. So Jesus was half heaven or eternal and half human. He came down and refused to sin, because he had a purpose: it was to be a "Lamb!" One that you can go to over and over and over again when you sin, not a covering but a cleansing or a shower from All sin always. Also it was not just for a year but for those that believe it cleanses a lifetime of sins. The Lord Jesus Christ is who paid the penalty for our sin with His death on the cross, he is our lamb! He is "The Lamb of God!"

43 - "Where Can I Hide?"

Can I escape God's presence? No, for there He is.

"There's nowhere to run to baby, nowhere to hide!" Does this sound familiar?

Where can you go where He is not? Nowhere, for God is there! The first astronauts that went to the moon, could they escape God's view? Could God not see their spaceship? Yes, God saw them, because He is there! Do you want to escape this life and hide in a cave underground? He's there! Do you want to head east or go west? He is there; as a matter of fact that is where he throws your sins when you ask forgiveness, remembering them no more! How far does east have to go to find west? Can I go on a cruise far away from land where there's no cell service? No, He is there too. Remember Jonah and the whale? Can you find the darkest spot in your attic and hide in an old army trunk? No, because God is light and He will sniff you out. Darkness runs from light every time! It reminds me of playing hide and seek with my dog. I hide and she uses her sense of smell to find me every time, even if I'm behind a closed door.

"For you created my inmost being; you knit me together in my mother's womb. Even before the ultra sound machine David says, "You saw me as my bones were being made"; I was not hidden from your sight in that sack of fluid, my secret place. You saw with your eyes my unformed body; my whole life's days were written in your book even before one of them came to be. I praise you; because I was thought about before you started me on the potter's wheel! Have you ever thought of just one aspect of God, when he made a

Labrador? Their sense of smell is nothing short of amazing: they can smell out a bone from a vacuum- packed bag hidden in Styrofoam peanuts, and then sealed in a heavy duty box coming through the mail. How about an ant's sense of smell? Have you ever laid down a lollipop on the ground and saw within an hour, every ant from a thirty mile radius came to get a lick. How did they know it was there when there was no ant in sight when you laid it down? Isn't it amazing?

I could go on and on at the endless qualities that God put in each one of us, even animals, to prove that He exists. God's Word says that when you come to Him in prayer, you must first believe He exists, that He is, and then know that when you pray, that He is a rewarder of those that seek Him. Since you can't escape from God, why not commit yourself to Him in relationship? Let God shine a searchlight of His powerful Word into your innermost thoughts and feelings, and by yielding yourself to be obedient to God's ways.

44 - The Royal Wedding

It was very interesting to me while I watched with the world, the grandest wedding of our day. The Royal Wedding! I listened as I heard some interesting things brought out by the interviewers. I heard them say that this couple wanted to live a common life. They did not want to be set apart, but wanted to blend in as ordinary people. They wanted to live a normal life, for the groom would not even wear a wedding ring. They took their own car and drove down the center strip breaking the protocol of royalty in a limousine. Now don't misunderstand me, I am not saying in the natural that this is not sweet. They did not want to stand out. They just wanted to relate to everyday people and break their protocol chains off.

I cannot help but see with my spiritual eyes a total different view. We are living in the last days and God is revealing things in the spirit to us. I saw the whole world watching as the royal blood couple stepped out of their divine birth poison to live the common lifestyle. They wanted to trade their birthright into eating a pot of stew, just for a moment to blend in with the common folks.

In a prophetic picture it is where the whole world is today. This royal position that God has given us is of a very high standard. 1 Peter 2:9 says, "But you are a chosen people, a Royal priesthood, a holy nation, God's special possession, that you may declare the praises of him who called you out of darkness into his wonderful light. "Once we have believed in Jesus the King, and invited him in our lives. We are of Royal birth; our blood line has been changed. Now we share in the riches in Christ, and are able to see clearly, because He has brought us into the light. We are set apart! We are not to blend in, but to live a HOLY life of a different kingdom.

He also says in a different place, "No one serving as a soldier gets entangled in civilian affairs, but rather tries to please his commanding officer."

Our wedding with Jesus will far outweigh what we saw on that day in April! "For the Wedding of the Lamb has come, and his bride has made herself ready. Fine linen, bright and clean, was given her to wear." Are you getting prepared to be the bride?" Revelation 19:7

The End!